Praise for Education for Transformation

"At a time when many educators are struggling wto find real and relevant ways to reach African American children and increase Black student achievement, Chike Akua, through Education for Transformation, has given us a powerful and practical blueprint. This book is a must-read for all serious educators who want to get results and understand the connection between culture and achievement."

      Joyce E. King, PhD.
      Benjamin E. Mays Chair of Urban Education
      Georgia State University

"Chike Akua and the work he produces represent the true Grio of our time. Education For Transformation *represents an important view of how to close the achievement gap for our most precious resources (our children)."*

      Dr. Bernadette Kelley, Chair
      State of Florida's African American History Task Force
      Florida A&M University

"Education for Transformation is a testament and a must read for those who want to recapture the essence of teaching and unlocking the natural genius in African American children. It empower teachers to see children as having the potential to demonstrate mastery."

      James C. Young, Ed.D.
      Professor and Coordinator for Teacher Education
      Clark Atlanta University

"Chike Akua has done a masterful job in his latest book, Education for Transformation. As one of his former student wrote, " most teachers teach from the book, but you teach from the heart."

> -Dr. Jawanza Kunjufu author of
> *There is Nothing Wrong with Black Students.*

"When I learned of the homegoing of Dr. Asa Hilliard, my heart ached. Not only had African people lost a scholar of epic proportion, but I worried that no one would be able to fill the void created by Dr. Hilliard's transitioning. Although my heart still aches for Dr. Hilliard —the man and the scholar; I Bless God for sending us the next intellectual warrior who will teach the 21st Century learner through the eyes of Africa's glorious past and present – Chike Akua! Move forward my brother and fulfill your destiny! "

> -Ako Kambon
> Visionary Leaders Institute

"Chike Akua's "Education for Transformation: The Keys to Releasing the Genius of African American Children *" will motivate even the mediocre teacher to work towards becoming a master in education. Akua is an inspiring author whose work exemplifies the fundamental importance of building relationships with students in order to help them understand the gifts that lie within them. It is refreshing to read the work of someone who has actually done it--made a difference for children."*

> -Stephen Peters, Ed & Author
>   *Choosing to Believe*
>   *Do You Know Enough About*
>   *Me to Teach Me?*

EDUCATION FOR TRANSFORMATION

The Keys to Releasing the Genius of African American Children

By

Chike Akua

Published by Imani Enterprises for the

www.MyTeacherTransformation.com

"Transforming Educators to transform Students to transform the World"

©2012 Chike Akua

ISBN 0-9704644-6-0

Other Books & DVDs by Chike Akua

*Sexceptional: The Ultimate
& Essential Teen Guide to Abstinence*
(2012)

African Sacred Science & Civilization DVD
(2007)

Reading Revolution: Reconnecting the Roots
(with Tavares Stephens)
(2006)

African Origins of Writing & Mathematics DVD
(2006)

*Words of Power: Ancient Insights & Modern Messages for
Parents, Teachers, and Students*
(2005)

A Kwanzaa Awakening: Lessons for the Community (4th Edition)
(2004)

The African Origins of Our Faith
(2004)

A Treasure Within: Stories of Remembrance & Rediscovery
(2001)

A Treasure Within: Parent/Teacher Resource Guide
(2001)

www.MyTeacherTransformation.com

**Standards-based, Research-driven
Culturally Relevant Instructional Strategies**

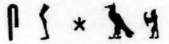

The Teacher Transformation Institute, (TTI) provides standards-based, research-driven, culturally relevant instructional strategies conferences for educators who work with African American students. Its purpose is to provide training to a new generation of teachers in African-centered and culturally relevant teaching techniques, thereby empowering teachers to transform the achievement culture in their schools and classrooms.

The vision is to create a teacher workforce that is culturally conscious, culturally competent, and deeply committed to creating centers of academic and cultural excellence.

Special Thanks

To my wife, Willette, for unwavering love and support.

To my sons, Jahbari and Amari, for inspiration and encouragement.

To my parents, Joseph and Faye Fenwick for the example of a Seba at home.

To Dr. Leslie Fenwick, Dr. James C. Young, Dr. Itihari Toure, for seeing the Seba in me

To Baba Ali & Mama Helen Salahuddin
and the Dzert Club African Genesis Institute

To Dr. Joyce E. King, and Dr. Hassimi Maiga
who serve, stand, shine, and teach to transform.

To Dr. Brian Williams and members of the Urban Educators Think Tank (UETT) at Georgia State University for giving scholarly feedback on this manuscript

To Perry Oliver of Interdenominational Theological Center (ITC) for reviewing this manuscript.

Dedication
(Literary Libation)

For Nana Baffour Amankwatia II (Dr. Asa G. Hilliard III),
Dr. Edward Robinson,
and the ancient and modern Seba who are
Ma'at Kheru. ("True of Voice").
Many thanks to those who have kept alive
the African tradition of excellence and achievement.

We will continue what you have begun.

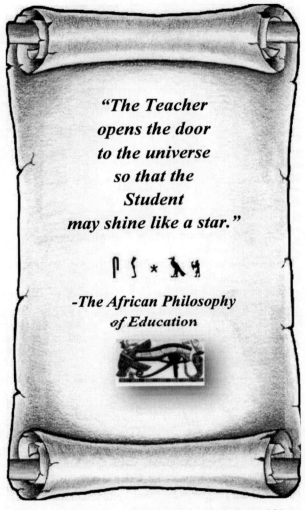

*"The Teacher
opens the door
to the universe
so that the
Student
may shine like a star."*

-*The African Philosophy
of Education*

**A scroll is a symbol of ancient wisdom. In ancient times. African scribes
would write their scientific discoveries and deep knowledge on papyrus
scrolls. These scrolls contained the wisdom of the ages and many still exist
today. Also in ancient times, the symbol of the Udjat (Third Eye) represented
deep insight. Every time you see a scroll and Udjat in this book, it contains
deep wisdom and insight for you to pause and think about.*

Contents

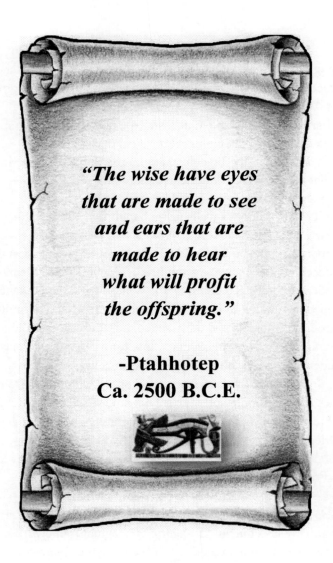

*"The wise have eyes
that are made to see
and ears that are
made to hear
what will profit
the offspring."*

**-Ptahhotep
Ca. 2500 B.C.E.**

Foreword

"It is said that "Good teachers don't do, they be." In keeping with this axiom, Chike Akua, himself a master teacher and recognized Teacher-of-the-Year, has laid out these ways of being. When followed, these master-teacher-ways-of-being simultaneously ignite an enthusiasm for teaching and learning even in the most challenging schools and classrooms.

Education for Transformation is an uplifting prescription for what ails too many American classrooms and schools -- disconnection. The book should be read by every person committed to children's well-being, happiness, intellectual growth, and academic success. Novice and veteran teachers alike will appreciate the book's solid advice which is grounded in the classroom experiences of a recognized Teacher-of-the-Year. Parents of school-aged children will benefit from the guidance provided about how to identify an engaging teacher and inviting classroom. Principals and other school administrators will be encouraged to grow schools that allow for more inspired master teachers like Akua who soar alongside students.

Education for Transformation opens with letters from Akua's former middle and high school students. These letters are vivid testimonies to the wisdom of integrating cultural knowledge and classroom instruction. If you read nothing else in the book be sure to read Xavier's story and Akua's 10 Nonverbal Questions Asked by All Students.

If you are fearful that you do not have the African-centered knowledge base that Akua has, abandon that fear. He perceptively lays out an Africentric conceptual framework and proven instructional methods for integrating the framework into everyday lessons and school-wide activities. His methods yield positive results for teacher and student and are applicable to all student populations. Akua is clear about the latter point: tapping into the students' cultural heritage -- in positive, knowledgeable, and strategic ways -- shifts the child's perception of self and community and is a powerful enabler of learning when done the right way.

Enjoy Education for Transformation! It succeeds in transporting the reader to a master teacher's vivid classroom and offers insights about how to craft such space and meaningfully connect with students in deep and lasting ways. When you finish reading this book, you will feel what all students feel when they are affirmed and well taught!"

Leslie T. Fenwick, PhD, Dean
Howard University School of Education

Preface

   Education for Transformation; Releasing the Genius in African American Students is a powerful and robust contribution to all who recognize that African American students have enormous abilities and untapped potential. Chike Akua, has effectively provided educators with an authentic and historic theory of change that builds on the legacy and zenith of the early African centers of education.

   Akua, reminds the reader, that African-centered education is foundational to the affirmative development and successful education of African American students. 'Every school district concerned with the academic, social and emotional achievement of these students should embrace this book without hesitation and make it a central component of their professional development agenda.' I am convinced that when teachers and other educators understand the genesis of "Seba", it will enable them to recognize, nurture and encourage the genius within our students.

          Ron Walker, Executive Director
          Coalition of Schools Educating Boys of Color
          (COSEBOC)

Introduction

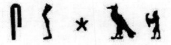

The earliest documented system of education had its genesis in the Nile Valley of Africa. Their system of education produced a people, a society, buildings, structures, monuments, and a high science whose sophistication has yet to be fully understood or surpassed (Hilliard, 1995).

In addition, the result of their system of education led to origins, innovations and expertise in reading and writing, language and literature, agriculture and astronomy, architecture and engineering, mathematics and medicine, philosophy and physics, science and technology, to name a few (Finch, 1998). The place was called Kemet and is today referred to as Egypt. Kemet was nourished and nurtured significantly, both culturally and spiritually, by its neighbor to the south, Nubia (Browder, 1992). It is in the Nile Valley of Africa that we encounter one of the first terms relative to teaching and learning—it is the word *seba*.

Seba, in the language of *medu netcher* (often referred to by the Greek term *hieroglyphics*) actually has three primary meanings: "teach," "door," "star" (Obenga, 2002). It is in the construction and connotation of this word that we find the ancient African philosophy of education and it is this—"The teacher opens the door to the universe, that the student may shine like a star."

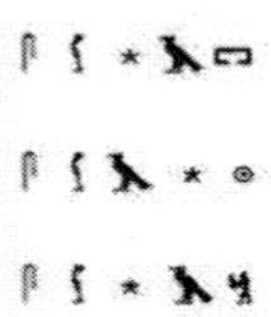

(seba) "door"

(seba) "star"

(seba) "teach", "teaching"

Seba came to refer also to the deep thought and wisdom of the wise and learned. The Master Teacher in ancient Kemet was often referred to as a *Seba* (Hilliard, 1997).

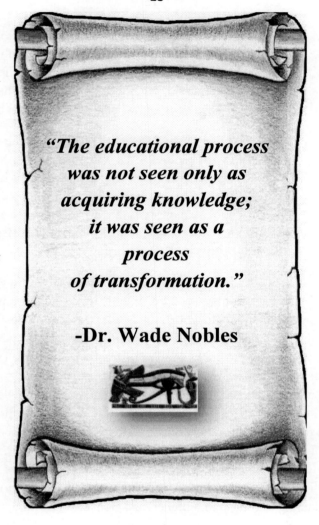

"The educational process was not seen only as acquiring knowledge; it was seen as a process of transformation."

-Dr. Wade Nobles

4500 years ago (2500 B.C.E.), the ancient teacher, sage, and scribe, Ptahhotep, who has written the oldest complete text in the world, gives us a definition of what a Seba does and what a Seba is known by:

The Seba (wise person/Master Teacher) feeds the Ka (soul) with what endures…the wise is known by his or her good actions. The heart of the wise matches his or her tongue and his or her lips are straight when he or she speaks. The wise have eyes that are made to see and ears that are made to hear what will profit the offspring (Hilliard, Williams, & Damali, 1987, p. 32).

In addition to this ambitious definition of what a teacher was, there was even a vast and distinct body of literature which instructed people in the way of the Master Teacher. The teachings were referred to as the *Sebait* (pronounced *say-by-eet*), wisdom texts or the books of wise instruction (Karenga, 1984). Wade Nobles observes that in ancient African schools, "the educational process was not seen only as acquiring knowledge; it was seen as a process of transformation of the learner or initiate, who progressed through successive stages of rebirth to become excellent" (Hilliard, Payton-Stewart, & Williams, 1990, p. 13). In addition to mastery of practical skills, this process was typified by the *whmy msw* (pronounced *we-he-mee me-su*), a re-awakening or rebirth into higher consciousness (Hilliard, 1997).

So this ancient African education was a cyclical process of initiation and transformation. When Nile Valley Africans migrated to west Africa, they reproduced the same philosophical conception of the nature of the child, the student, and each child's potential (Maiga, 2008). Each child was seen as a rising

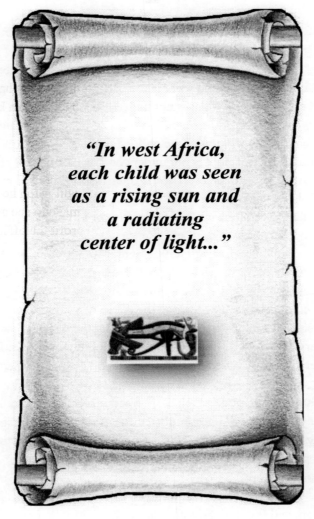

*"In west Africa,
each child was seen
as a rising sun and
a radiating
center of light..."*

sun and a radiating center of light with tremendous power and energy (Fu-Kiau, 1991).

The Kemetic description of the ancient Master Teacher is not only a far cry from what is expected of teachers today, it is based in a philosophy that is not understood or illuminated in most western schools of education where teachers are trained. In addition, the description of the child/student as a rising sun and radiating center of light is not understood or illuminated either. In short, those who teach African American children, in most cases, have not consulted either our most traditional and consistent ancient examples of expertise or our most contemporary examples of excellence.

Now, fast-forward 4500 hundred years from the ancient to the modern. In the first essay of *Young, Gifted and Black: Promoting High Achievement Among African-American Students*, Theresa Perry located the African American philosophy of education. After examining the writings of Frederick Douglass, Harriett Jacobs, Malcolm X, Ben Carson, Joycelyn Elders, Gwendolyn Parker, Haki Madhubuti, Septima Clark, and Maya Angelou, a definite pattern with conscious consistency emerged: a theme of "freedom for literacy and literacy for freedom, racial uplift, citizenship, and leadership" (Perry, Steele, & Hilliard, 2003, p. 10). Then, as now, "the purpose of education is to secure the survival of a people" (Wilson, 1992, p. 1).

In other words, the purpose of education was to secure freedom and freedom brought with it the right to a proper education. Education inculcated within the student a responsibility to improve the plight of one's people. It is the underlying ethos and essence of the pursuit of education for Black people in America. However, the African American philosophy of education is not isolated—rather, it is a clear and

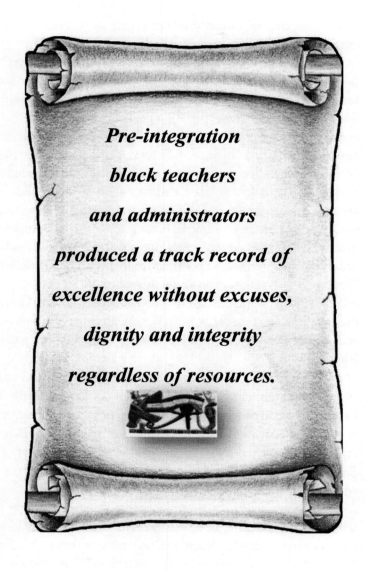

Pre-integration

black teachers

and administrators

produced a track record of

excellence without excuses,

dignity and integrity

regardless of resources.

compelling cultural thread in a broader tapestry, an extension of the ancient African philosophy of education.

Education and socialization have always been a top priority for African people whether in ancient and independent times or in the context of *maafa*, the intentional, catastrophic interruption of African civilization characterized by enslavement, colonization, castration, miseducation, economic manipulation, lynching, rape, family separation, etc.(Ani, 1980).

Prior to integration, even in the midst of dilapidated buildings, a diabolically unequal distribution of funds, and second hand textbooks, the desire for and pursuit of education was clear and consistent among black people. In addition, parent meetings were packed with care-givers who insisted on the best education and preparation possible for their children (Siddle-Walker, 2000). Those who know this narrative sit in awe, wonder, disappointment, and disillusionment when examining the state of education for African Americans today. If this standard of excellence was the case prior to integration, what happened?

There is another story. There is a little known narrative as to why far too many of our schools are not producing the excellence we expect or desire. With the onset of integration, many white educational leaders in the 1960s and 1970s, in an effort to skirt the mandates of the 1954 *Brown v. Board of Education* decision, began to get rid of black teachers and administrators.

Today, over 70% of urban school teachers are white and female in schools where students are overwhelmingly children of color (Fenwick, 2001). Many teachers today exhibit what Joyce King calls dysconscious racism, an uncritical habit of mind that accepts the status quo as a given (King, 1991). Because of the inherent, uncritical acceptance of inequity, dysconsciousness prevents the active pursuit of social justice. It creates more than apathy; it creates cooperation with educational oppression. However, pre-integration black teachers and administrators produced a track record of excellence without excuses, dignity and integrity regardless of resources, and a curricular thrust toward cultural excellence and social justice (Siddle-Walker, 2000).

> "The powerful will never educate the powerless to take their power from them."
> -Dr. John Henrik Clarke

In the wake of the *Brown* decision, the black teacher workforce was decimated. Over 39,000 black teachers and leaders were the victims of "dismissals, demotions, forced resignations, 'non-hiring', token promotions, reduced salaries and diminished responsibilities" (Fultz, 2004, p. 14). The ranks of African American teachers and administrators "has declined to less than half of what it was before integration (Hilliard, 1997, p. 60.).

All of this was done in the name of complying with the *Brown* decision. However, it led one informant to note that it is "not integration, rather it is *disintegration*" (Fultz, 2004, p. 14). Indeed black schools slowly disintegrated along with the high standards of achievement. In light of this, it is important to note that today, the low number of African American teachers is not accidental, but *intentional*. Perhaps this is why John Henrik Clarke notes with sober and systematic incisiveness that "the powerful will never educate the powerless to take their power from them" (Clarke, 1991, p. 18).).

Black children were sent to "integrated" schools which did not foster the ancient African or African American philosophy of education. By and large, their caring teachers who demanded excellence without excuses were

"*The powerful
will never educate
the powerless
to take their power
from them.*"

-Dr. John Henrik Clarke

no longer present. As a result, over the past several decades, African American children have been sliding down a slippery slope resulting in alien identity and underachievement. The 2010 Schott State Report on Black Males in Education indicated that the national black male graduation rate was a mere 47% (Jackson, 2010). Some school systems had Black male graduation rates as low as an appalling 22%. Moreover, many urban schools are struggling with increased incidents of classroom management problems and violence. Clearly, the current system of public education is not working.

This book is for those who wish to recapture the ancient African and African American philosophy of educational excellence and effectively put it into practice. This book is about results.

This is the backdrop against which many teachers enter the teacher workforce. Many enter the workforce not knowing what caused the seemingly daunting day-to-day challenges they face trying to reach and teach children in urban schools. Experienced and veteran teachers often watch the year-to-year erosion of any semblance of excellence. Often the children and their parents are blamed without a contextualized understanding of the socio-cultural forces that have been imposed upon them.

But even with these devastating challenges, many African American schools, teachers, and students have upheld the standard of excellence that was once so common. Unfortunately, their stories are not often enough used as examples of what is possible.

This book is for those who are interested in solutions that are far beyond minimal competency tests. It is for those who understand that systemic certification and college degrees are not enough. It is for those who wish to recapture the ancient African and African American philosophy of education and effectively put it into practice. This is education for transformation. It is this tradition "that made us respected as teachers all over the globe" (Gallman, Ani & Williams, 2003, p. 61). This book is about results. It is about my transformational experiences of attempting to recapture and reproduce the ancient African and African American philosophy of education and putting it into practice in my almost 20 years as an educator.

> "I have taught in situations where 22 out of 24 of my homeroom students had a parole officer.

For those educators reading this book who teach mixed populations of students, who may be wondering if the methods described here are too ethnically centered, please be mindful of the thoughtful words of Carol Lee, "Once we learn to teach poor Black children, we will likely learn better how to educate all children" (King, 2005, p. xxvi).

I have taught in urban schools and suburban schools, predominantly black schools and schools with mixed populations and diversity. I have taught high-achieving students on the accelerated track and students who were below grade level, students whose behavior was exemplary and students whose behavior and socialization required acute and immediate attention, intervention, and modification. I have also taught students labeled with every undesirable initial one can think of. I have taught in situations where 22 out of 24 of my homeroom students had a parole officer.

In addition, I have had the opportunity to travel around the country speaking at conferences and coaching teachers and leaders in public, charter, and private schools. I have spoken at

ℙ ʃ ⋆ 𝕜 ५

parent meetings and school assemblies for students, addressing hundreds of students at a time in some of the most challenged communities and challenging schools. I have observed that there are startling and crippling similarities in America's public schools relative to the achievement of black children. But there is good news. The challenges many teachers and schools are facing can be repaired . Hilliard notes, "Evaluation research shows that extraordinarily high achievement gains can be made, in a relatively brief period, by relatively simple approaches, in spite of typical challenges, for the lowest income students, regardless of race" (Perry, Hilliard, & Steele, p. 144).

This book begins with "The voice of the Children," the testimony of those touched firsthand by education for transformation. Then, the philosophical foundation which undergirds education for transformation is examined. The philosophical foundation is fundamental to understanding the nature and needs of African American children. This followed by the practical application of the philosophical foundation.

So what follows are the methods that I have found to be effective in educating African American students. These are not only methods I developed—more than anything they are methods I have observed, adopted, and adapted from other effective educators in the passionate pursuit of teaching my students. These methods are grounded in ancient African and African American philosophy and practices. Of course, many aspects of what will be shared here also have universal application. In my estimation and experience, in order to produce academic and cultural excellence, what follows is not optional, but *essential*.

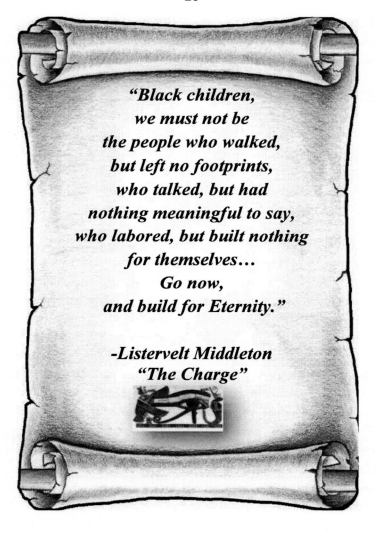

"Black children,
we must not be
the people who walked,
but left no footprints,
who talked, but had
nothing meaningful to say,
who labored, but built nothing
for themselves…
Go now,
and build for Eternity."

-Listervelt Middleton
"The Charge"

Chapter 1

The Voice of the Children

Ρ ∫ *

"Mr. Akua...most teachers teach from the book, but you teach from the heart."

                    -Chanel (7ᵗʰ Grade)

Ρ ∫ * ⱶ ¥

At the end of every school year, I would write my students a letter on the board. The letter would read something like this:

Dear Brothers & Sisters:

It has been a privilege and a blessing to teach you this year. I hope you remember the lessons from the Book of Life more so than the textbook. I know you will leave here and do great things. I know you will transform the world into a place of peace for all and make the Ancestors proud. Have a safe and blessed summer.

In Spirit & Truth,

Mr. Akua

I would then have my students write me a letter after they completed their final exam. They had to tell me the most important thing they learned over the course of the year. It did not have to be an academic lesson, it could be a life lesson that they learned and felt was important. I gave them this assignment for two reasons: 1) I felt it was important for them to reflect on all they had learned over the course of the year 2) I wanted to know what impacted them most about *how* I taught and *what* I taught.

Through the fourteen years I spent teaching and even during my student teaching, I saved many of the letters my students wrote to me. One of the things I think teachers need most today along with effective training is *encouragement*. These letters can help fill that void. It will also illustrate the incredible impact teaching has. It is difficult to see it during the day-to-day challenges. At some point of discouragement, every teacher asks him/herself, "Why am I doing this? Am I really making a difference?" I found that Spirit often answered this inquisitive prayer by sending a student to me who would tell me I was making a difference, or they would write me a letter expressing the same sentiment. Reading these letters helped to lift my spirits on many occasions and remind me why we do what we do.

You may be surprised by how articulate some of these letters are. *Don't be.* Again, what our children are capable of is extraordinary. These letters are from a cross-section of my students, not just the ones who excelled academically. Our children have a great deal to say when we take the time to listen. In addition to the letters from students, there is also a letter from a parent. Some students also contacted me when they got to high school and some even 10-15 years later.

Dear Mr. Akua:

In all of our lives we come across people who inspire and teach us in miraculous, unimaginable ways. You are one of those people to me! You are one of few examples of what appears to be a well put together man who has both purpose and unlimited promise. I can only hope that I can aid my younger brother in becoming a person with your values, insight, knowledge, and mentality.

If throughout your teaching career you ever feel as if you may not be making a difference, re-read this card. I have spoken with faculty and staff from administration to guidance about you. Everyone has the utmost respect for you and wish all the best for you. The pupils that you have taught have also been inspired by you. Some students who have never enjoyed English or other people's cultures now are eagerly anticipating learning more.

What have you done for me? You have introduced me to a new awareness. I have for a long time had a problem with authoritative figures. The knowledge that you gave to me allows me to now recognize this problem, among others, and search for ways to ameliorate them. In my search for Oneness with God, you have been a tool through which knowledge and, more importantly, wisdom has been gained.

It has been said that if you make a difference in one person's life that you have conquered the world. You have definitely made the right choice [to become a teacher]-not that you doubted this at any moment-and should continue to serve mankind by spreading your knowledge to its children.

I wish you all of the good fortune that you deserve. There should be more teachers in this world who truly want to make a difference and are interested in being instructors instead of babysitters. I will continue to pray for you and ask that you do the same [for me]. Hopefully, my little brother will be inspired by an African American man like you and also achieve greatness. Have a happy graduation and a wonderful, fulfilling life.

Camisha(12th Grade)

(from my 6-week high school student teaching experience)

Mr. Akua,

I will understand if you do not remember me, but my name is Tirrell D. I had the distinct pleasure of having you educate me at Stephenson Middle School during the 1998-1999 school year.

To be very honest, I was web browsing recently and decided to type in your name. What I found was nothing short of amazing. I was so inspired to see that the Language Arts teacher that I looked up to so much in 7th grade is doing so much good in the world. I will not hesitate to say that you are one of the reasons why I went to college and majored in Education.

Today I teach 9th grade College Prep and Honors students at Mill Creek High School. I just wanted to send you an email and say that not only have you impacted my life in a major way, but I also use lessons and ideals you taught me over 10 years ago in my classroom.

Tirrell D.

Hi Mr. Akua:

My name is Brittany Stewart. I was in your 7th grade class at Stephenson Middle School. You taught me reading and English a few years ago. I am now a senior at Stephenson High School. I hope that you remember who I am because you were someone I could never forget! You have made such an impact on my life and the lady that I have become! I just wanted to thank you for all of the wonderful things that you have given to me!

I can remember conversations alone that forced me to do better, to want better and to know that I deserve better. To me you are the ideal person, the perfect role model for anyone, young or old. You are so giving and ask for nothing in return. I know I have a lot to learn and still quite young to the world, but I feel as though I have an advantage because I had you as a teacher.

I am not sure yet about what school I plan on attending but I know I plan to major in education so I can have as big of an impact on someone's life as you did on mine. I love you so much and consider it a blessing to have known you!

Brittany S.

P.S. I forgot to thank you for the confidence you have given me because it has truly made a difference!

Dear Mr. Akua:

It has been a pleasure having you as a teacher throughout this year. You taught me how to deal with certain situations and how to be a better person, in general. I will take this knowledge with me, use it, and spread it among many people. I've learned to "display my intelligence, not my ignorance," how to get into the proper mindset to learn, and how to handle responsibility. Those are the important things in life.

This has been my best year in school, maybe not grade-wise, but in learning wisdom and not as much book knowledge. Our relationship went past student-teacher, but to father-son and friend to friend. I appreciate that. You know I have no father. It's a joy when I can talk and chill with a teacher and picture him being my father.

You gave me the key to my past and future, but now I must open it and explore the things in it. All the things you taught about Black history were and are not taken for granted by me. I enjoyed learning that the most. One quality you have is that you are always ready to learn, even from a student. When somebody has that attitude, I am glad to be able to associate with them.

Your Student,
Philip(7th grade)

Dear Mr. Akua: *June, 1993*

I really don't know what to say. Words cannot express how I feel. You have done so much for me. I can never repay you. You were there for me when people made me cry and made me feel bad about myself. You helped me learn about who I am.

When I first came here, all the girls except me thought you and Mr. Rogers were really fine. I just couldn't see it. I thought that something was wrong with me. And I still don't think you and him are fine. But you have to be the most intelligent man I have gotten to know. You know where you have come from and never once forgot that. You also know where you are going. You have set a terrific example for your students and you should be very proud of yourself. Next to Mrs. Price, you are my favorite teacher. And out of all of my teachers, I will miss you two the most. I don't think I'll ever encounter two teachers that I love more than you and Mrs. Price. I'll miss you when I'm in high school, but I'll never forget you. Thanks for everything.

P.S. Tell your fiancé she is a very lucky woman and not to let you go or I'll set you up with my Aunt Ann. I would love to have you for an uncle!

Christy (8th grade)

Dear Mr. Akua: *November, 1993*

Asta lama lakeum [As-salaam alaikum: Arabic for "peace be unto you." Kamau thought I was Muslim]. I know that I'll never be able to finish school. Because I want to learn but because of my Dad giving me mental and sometimes physical abuse, my mom is going to try and get me to see a school psychologist because it is stopping me from learning a bit. That is why I get angry so quick. But I'm sorry for snapping at you. Do I need to make up any assignments?

Your favorite 4th period student,

Kamau (8th grade)

Kamau wrote me ten years later. His emailed letter as an adult is below.

Dear Mr. Akua:

It was by God's grace that I was able to locate you using Yahoo web search. It has been 10 years since I was in your class at Hines Middle School located in Newport News, Virginia. I am writing this letter to let you know just how much being in your class 10 years ago changed my life and made me a better person. I am now 24 and I have two beautiful daughters: Dianna and Aaliyah. Their ages are 5 and 3. I am currently a student at Thomas Nelson Community college. I am transferring to Old Dominion University in the fall to get a degree in education.

I distinctly remember being in your class, being a clown, disruptive, and sometimes ignorant of my choice of words and how and when I used them affected others. I remember when you would say, "Kamau, I need you to stay after class. I just knew I was being written up. But your methods of discipline didn't result in being sent to the principal's office.

You had a better punishment: an informative discussion. At my age now, I no longer see those discussions as punishment. It was those discussions that in the end made me the man who now loves life and cherishes every moment of it. My story 10 years ago was that I had a father that left me when my mother decided to get a divorce. I never had a father figure after that. Before the divorce took place,

In the end I would act out and cut up in school just to get a rise out of my peers. At the time I didn't know the value of an education. I do now and it's because of a teacher that really made me understand that I could do anything I put my mind to. Sadly, some students that were in my class that didn't take warning to your words and are either in jail, dead, or strung out on drugs. I saw to it that I would not become a statistic, because I had the guidance of an educator who showed me that the path I was going would make me end up in one of those places.

Eventually I would end up losing focus of the tasks at hand which were my studies at school. I used acting out as a way to suppressing my problems at home. But you saw through it like glass even though you maybe never experienced what I had been going through. You made me see the bigger picture: that the actions of my parents, and the knowledge from an educator would define who I would become.

I learned the true meaning of the words "knowledge of self." This is a process when you read books to learn about things to gain knowledge for personal reasons—to define your ancestry and African American heritage. A teacher once said, "Not everything in these textbooks is accurate, but it's up to you as an individual to find out the real deal on your own."

I just want to say thank you for the opportunity to be a student in your class and learn how to become a young man. It is because of you, Mr. Akua, that I chose a career as an educator. You were an inspiring educator that actually cared and loved your students as your own children. You never gave up on us, even the students who acted out like me.

I want to become a leader for black youth. Someone has to show them that there's more to life than driving a Hummer, selling drugs to our own people, and having kids at a young age. I just want you to know that you do make a difference and I appreciate all that you taught me as a youth 10 years ago. I had thoughts as a youth that you didn't care and you put up with me for a paycheck. In all actuality, you really did care and it shows through me and this letter. I stand here before you humbly to say that because of you, Mr. Akua, I am a better young black man and human being.

Peace and Blessings,

Kamau

Dear Mr. Akua:

First, I am going to miss you very much. This was my favorite class and you were my favorite teacher. Though all the work you gave us seemed like a lot, in the end it was nothing. We got so used to it. I truly enjoyed every minute of your class. You made me use my mind more than I used to. You always challenged me, as well as the others. I loved the journal topics. I'm sure you noticed because I always raised my hand to read mine.

I know as well as the Lord that you were my teacher for a reason. You taught me how to show my intelligence instead of my ignorance. This summer, I am going to make a priority to write a journal. I loved learning about the Third Eye, about how we can rely on help from our Ancestors, and the poems we learned. The one I liked the most was "The Clock of Destiny" [also called "God's Minute" by Benjamin E. Mays]. I can relate to this one the most. I only have a short time here and it is up to me to make the best of it. I did hope that somehow you could be our teacher again next year. But it is only fair that you have to teach all of your knowledge to others that will be rising up to 7th grade.

I will remember all the material you taught me and use it in everyday life. I just pray that next year I have a teacher as challenging as you are. The children you have next year, I hope they respect you for all you are going to do for them. Thanks for being here for us and showing me my Higher Self. I learned a lot from the Book of Life and will always cherish it.

I was truly blessed to have you as my 7th grade language arts teacher.

Ursula (7th grade)

Dear Mr. Akua,

The most important thing I learned this year was that <u>all</u> people, especially Black people should know about Black History because Black History is beautiful. I learned so many fascinating things about my African heritage and many famous African American brothers and sisters. What makes this information so important is that during all my other years of education this information was denied me.

And I really thank you, Mr. Akua, for really opening my eyes so I could see how great of a people we are. I promise you, Mr. Akua, that I will hold all of this knowledge dear to my heart and never forget you because you are the best teacher I've had and will probably ever have. I will take the knowledge you have given me and help my Black brothers and sisters, and even the world. I thank you once again, Mr. Akua, and I love you.

P.S. I'm really going to make you proud of me.

Love,

Daryl B. (7th grade)

*A letter from Daryl's mother is on the next page.

*Daryl calls me at least 2-3 times per year to check in. He graduated from Holy Cross as a student athlete with a degree in Political Science and a minor in African American Studies. He is working in Milwaukee and plans to earn a law degree.

Dear Mr. Akua,

 I have planned to write this letter several times during the course of this school year, but after Jerry's funeral, I could not allow another day to pass without letting you know how much of an impact you have made on Daryl's life. After today, again I realize how important it is to share and thank those who bless you and your loved ones' lives.

 Mr. Akua, when you breathe out—Daryl takes that breath in. He comes home everyday and verbatim shares with me your lesson for the day. Your knowledge and teaching skills fill and challenge his mind. He has shown a thirst for learning and retaining that I have not seen before. And I love it!! Daryl has even shared some of your teaching skills with one of my friends that is a teacher and she plans to use these techniques in her classroom.

 Mr. Akua, it is obvious to me that you are walking in your anointing. As you continue to bless and feed the minds and lives of young people, your blessings will overflow. You are an instrumental part of our young people's future and to this I say, "Thank you!"

 The majority of my life is focused around Daryl, but I feel he is worth it. Raising him to be the man of God that he is to become is not an assignment that I take lightly. I am aware that Daryl has a special anointing upon his life and I feel blessed to have him as my son. I am often told by others that I give too much of myself to him and that I do nothing for me. But, Mr. Akua, as far as I am concerned, there is no such thing! The experience today [Jerry's funeral] confirmed that. I feel that I have five short years left [before Daryl goes to college] to pour into Daryl the morals and values of life that he will need to become what God has destined. This is not a lot of time.

 Mr. Akua, Daryl shared with me what you told him when he came to comfort you [after the funeral]. As a single mother raising a teenage son, you have no idea how much that meant to me—and to Daryl! We were both very flattered. You are the *second male role model that has said that to him. Thank you for making a difference in my son's life.*

I am aware of some circumstances that Daryl shared with you and the advice/comments that you provided. Each time it was confirmation of what I had previously said to him. I know this is the beginning of a difficult decision-making stage of Daryl's life and although we are close, he is at a time in life that he needs positive male role models that he can identify with. I hope that you will be available for Daryl to consult with you after the school year is over.

Mr. Akua, you are the type of man that I hope Daryl will become. Stephenson Middle School is very blessed to have you and other teachers like you as instructors at the school. Keep up the good work! It matters and is greatly appreciated!

God's continued blessings upon you and your family.

Thank You,

Yolanda B.
(Mother of Daryl B.)

Dear Mr. Akua:

> *Hi. This is Mia, your favorite student in the whole world. Just playing (unless I really am). Thank you for being my teacher. You were my favorite teacher this year. I've learned a lot in your class that will help me in my life. I will use my higher consciousness more often because of you. When I am older, I will pass on most of your teachings and advice to my children.*
> *Thank you for being a good teacher, not just to me but to all of your students. I am proud to call you my teacher and the only thing I regret is you couldn't teach more students in our school to raise their higher consciousness. I am truly blessed to have you in my life.*

P.S. I can see you years from now reading these letters from us.

Mia (7th grade)

Dear Mr. Akua:

*I have enjoyed all the days that I've been in your class. I have learned so much. Not only have you been a teacher, but an inspiration, as well. You have not been a boring teacher because **most teachers teach from the book, but you teach from the heart.** I loved coming to your class each day, but now that it is coming to an end I will miss you and the things you teach. What I will remember most about the class is what our Ancestors had to go through.*

I have learned things that I never heard about. It hurts to see the walls of the classroom now [at the end of the school year] because they are bare. I hope you remember me even though I have not been a top student in grades. But keep me in your heart and I'll keep you in mine. You will always be remembered by me and many others. I hope your summer will be filled with joy and happiness and I'll see you next year.

Chanel (7th grade)

Dear Mr. Akua:

I am going to miss you. I will not be here next year. I have had a lot of fun in this class. I liked the way you taught us to look deeper into ourselves. You taught us how to use the Third Eye. I liked playing the basketball and football review game. You taught us that everything has a deeper meaning. We will take your advice and follow the road that has been less traveled on [an allusion to the poem by Robert Frost that we had studied]. By taking this road, maybe it will open new doors for us.

I will follow my dream to become an anesthesiologist. I did well in this class only because I had a great teacher and I was determined to succeed. I have displayed my ignorance sometimes and I regret that. I will continue to display my intelligence. It has been a pleasure being with you.

This summer I am going to New Jersey and Alabama. I also plan on serving God better. I am one of Jehovah's Witnesses. Farewell. Wherever I go I will think of your quote, "Display your intelligence, not your ignorance."

Brandon (7th grade)

Dear Mr. Akua:

It has been a pleasure and an honor being in your class this year. You have taught me so many things about life mentally and spiritually. I hope that as I get older and wiser the quotes you gave us continue to help me through my days. I will never forget you because you opened up a new level of the world for me. I also hope that you will never forget me although I know it would be kinda hard since at times I acted a little silly in class. People always say that the first impression you make on someone will be a lasting impression to them. So I hope that my first impression to you was good because I want the last one to be good also.

People say that English is a boring subject. Mr. Akua, I loved your class because you did not make it boring, but you made it fun. Mr. Akua, I hope I continue to be in your heart as you will continue to be in mine. I hope you continue to bless kids as you have blessed me through your teachings. Some of your students said you were too serious, but I always knew you were about business and education because you know how hard it is for a Black person to make it in this world. I hope you accomplish all your goals in life and I know you hope I will accomplish mine.

Meghan (7th grade)

Mr. Akua:

I was very lucky to have you as a teacher this year. My social studies teacher has much Black self-hatred. She tells us schools like Howard University and other historically Black colleges aren't good schools. But you have told us that Black colleges produce more than great minds, they produce tomorrows [an allusion to a Black college poster in my classroom]. You've always been there to fill in the gap and correct mis-information about Black people, even though you're a language arts teacher. This is what I will remember most about this year.

Everyone on Team 7B is fortunate to have you as a teacher. People on other teams have read about you [in community newpapers and magazines] and wanted you as a teacher. I even know a girl who tried to switch teams so she could have you as a teacher. You are a very gifted teacher and I will miss you.

Ashley (7th grade)

Dear Mr. Akua:

Some of the things I will remember about this class will be the fun we had on our presentations. I will also always remember the knowledge you shared with us, opening our Third Eye and awakening our Spirits.

I believe more teachers should be like you. I liked all the proverbs and morals posted around the room in your "Temple of Higher Learning" [a reference to a point I made to the class that my room was not a classroom, but ' a Temple of Higher Learning' and that they needed to govern themselves accordingly]. In your class I liked doing journal entries, analyzing poems, cartoons [satirical/political comic strips], and quotes. It was just a pleasure having you as my mentor and helping me when I needed it. I also learned a lot about you when I interviewed you.

Your Mentoree:

Rashad ("one guided to the right with good conduct")(7th Grade)

Dear Mr. Akua:

It has been a pleasure and a blessing being with you this year. I as a person have truly found my inner self. You taught things about people, yourself, our souls, and how we must be true to ourselves as well as to other people. You made me realize that everyone has a journey in life. And that there will be hard times, but we must try hard, keep going and never give up. This year in English has been very different than my past English classes. And I thank you for that.

Things I didn't know about life just struck me. You taught us about life itself. Instead of teaching us straight from the books, you taught us about our past, our Ancestors and how we got here. You showed us how they [our Ancestors] struggled and tried hard to get us where we are today. And now it is our turn to show the world what we can do because we are today's future and tomorrow lies within us. I hope you have a nice summer. God bless you.

Shambrina (7th grade)

Dear Mr. Akua:

During this school year in your class, you taught me about my heritage. You are like no other teacher I have ever had. Although you teach language arts, you also helped us open our Third Eye and you explained our roots to us through language arts. You are like two teachers rolled up into one: a language arts teacher and a Black history teacher.

I enjoyed when you taught us about our Ancestors and where we came from through books and videos. You always told our class to display our intelligence not our ignorance. Now we realize that ignorance was never a part of our heritage and never should be. In your class, class is never boring because I know that when I walk through the door of your classroom I will learn more about myself and my people as a whole.

Nanika (7th grade)

Dear Mr. Akua:

This year you have been a very good teacher. While doing things like going to the movies I will take what you taught me into consideration. The thing I will remember most about this class is how you never accepted less than our best. We were always told that we knew things we just had to pull them out and to display our intelligence and not our ignorance.

Your words of wisdom will stay in my mind much longer than any poem we read or story we talked about. Through the year you also taught us to know ourself. Now that I know myself I can be true to myself. Anybody can teach someone something, but when you put emphasis on what you say and they are positive things, that makes a difference, and to me you have made a difference.

Trevis (7th grade)

Mr. Akua:

Thank you. Thank you for being the wonderful teacher that you are and always will be. I can honestly say that you have been my favorite and most inspiring teacher. You know what? I've actually learned something-lots! I learned about our Ancestors, our Third Eye, and much more. Even though you're as hard on us as I don't know what and stay on us 24-7, I know you do it because you love us and only want the best.

I'm going to try to keep all the good conversations and kind words that you gave us. Even as this year comes to an end, our knowledge continues. You know why? Because "the knowledge of the Universe is meticulously woven into the very fabric of my being. And all I have to do is pull out the refreshing waters of infinite insight [a reference to another quote which reads: "My soul is a well from which I can draw the refreshing waters of infinite insight."]. Even though my grades didn't always show it, I really have learned a lot. Thanks!

Candice (7th grade)

*Candice is now an elementary school teacher.

Dear Mr. Akua:

It has truly been a blessing being in your class this year. This class has really ministered to my heart and helped me to be all that I can be. Under no circumstances do I want to leave your class, but as we all know, life must go on and now it's someone else's turn to be as blessed as we all have been this year. It's so hard to find a strong Black Christian teacher but it soothes my soul to know that there are more African kings like you out there.

A letter can only say so much and honestly words cannot express the way I feel. Jaguar Bible Study has opened up a new world for others and I hope that you continue to minister to others as I will do the same. [Breyana was the founder of JBS. She wrote a letter to the principal requesting that students be able to have Bible study in the morning before school. She requested that I be the faculty advisor to the club].

Though my literature has not yet been fully recognized, when I become famous, I won't forget you. Though I've been writing since a young age, you have truly opened up the focus on a deeper meaning in life. Unlike some teachers, I can truly say that you really do care. You're open on discussions and you're real, meaning you don't deprive us of any knowledge. You're not afraid to show your faith in any way and you've taught us to display our intelligence and not our ignorance.

Life itself has truly changed for me this year in coming to your class. Keep teaching, believing, and praying because prayer changes things. You're a good man and Lord knows it's hard to find a truly good man. You've taught me that statistics don't make a person, the person makes the statistics. Even though I've never met your wife, I'm sure that she is very proud of your accomplishments.

Keep publishing books and don't forget me because when my book is published your name will be there. Answer to your callings and don't let anyone stop you because remember, one day you will have a child of your own to give the same understanding that you have given to us. The year is coming to an end and yet it's so sad to go. This letter can only tell you so much. Even if you don't remember me, please remember one thing: "Keep God first!" So now as we sadly depart, I'll close my letter, but never my heart!

May life bring you love, peace, and may your blessings overflow,

Breyana (7th Grade)

The last time I spoke to Breyana (a couple of years ago when she called) , she was in her third year at Howard University Law School.

Dear Mr. Akua:

The things I remember most about this class are the things that helped me change in some type of way. Like the times you stressed us about finishing our work and how it would affect us in the future. The lessons you taught really let us know you cared. You also taught me to take leadership and responsibility for my generation and to make the Ancestors proud.

The quotes you kept repeating and repeating—I'm glad you did it because they made me open my Third Eye which I didn't even know I had. So if no one else tells you this, you're hearing it from me. I'm glad I had the chance to be in your class because you made a path for me that I will follow in a way that I cannot explain. So I thank you for everything this year.

Amina (7th grade)

*The last time I spoke to Amina(about nine months ago), she was completing the last semester of her Masters degree in Engineering at the University of Alabama, Huntsville. She had called to invite me to present"African Sacred Science" to the Minority Graduate Student Association.

Dear Mr. Akua:

You have been a big influence on me. As I go through these rough times, I will always remember those quotes you told me and those five steps to stay in balance. That makes me want to become a better man and take a better stand in what I want to become. Your teaching in JBS (Jaguar Bible Study) helped me, too. It helped me get myself in touch with you spiritually.

When we played basketball you taught me a lot of things. But I know I taught you a lot of things on the court (smile). I hope one day you can catch up with me and be on my level in basketball. But I don't think you ever will. Have a great summer.

Brandon C. (7th grade

Questions for Thought, Reflection & Discussion

1. What are some common themes in these letters?
2. Is there a particular letter that stands out to you? Which one(s)? Why?
3. What do you think these children experienced that made them write such letters?

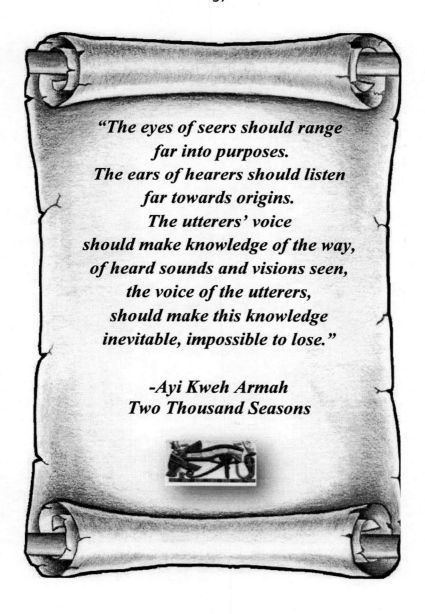

"The eyes of seers should range
far into purposes.
The ears of hearers should listen
far towards origins.
The utterers' voice
should make knowledge of the way,
of heard sounds and visions seen,
the voice of the utterers,
should make this knowledge
inevitable, impossible to lose."

-Ayi Kweh Armah
Two Thousand Seasons

Chapter 2

Opening the Way:

Creating a Climate for Excellence

Uncommon accomplishments require uncommon commitment. These five magic words encapsulate the essence of what it takes for teachers, leaders, faculties, and school systems today that desire to be effective. The commitment that is needed to get all students to achieve is one that goes far beyond what most school systems desire or require. Master teachers often come in early and stay late. They are never satisfied with what they already know. They are always seeking to extend their knowledge and expose their students to new information, experiences, and skills, even when the school or school system they teach in does not demand it.

> "Creating a transformative experience for your students begins with creating an inviting, transformative environment."

Creating a transformative experience for your students begins with creating an inviting, transformative environment. Several years ago when I was teaching eighth grade, a parent examined my classroom a few days before the school year began. She had come up to the school after hours to look at all the classrooms on the eighth grade hall. After examining my classroom, she made a beeline for the principal's office.

"What teacher is in Room 211?" she demanded.

"That's Mr. Akua," replied the principal proudly, but a bit concerned. "Why do you ask?"

"I want my son in his class."

"Why?" asked the principal.

"I just walked through his classroom. It's the way his classroom is set up… and the pictures he has on the wall—that's the environment I want my son in."

> "...I could not find the images I was looking for at the local teacher's store."

When my principal told me this story, I smiled. What this parent was referring to was the clear, culturally affirming pictures, the inspiring and encouraging quotes and proverbs posted in the room. She felt the spirit of the environment I was trying to create without me even being there. When students walk into my room on the first day of school, they look around in awe and wonder soaking up every bit of energy infused in the pictures, posters, and bulletin boards. Your room, whether you're there or not has a particular kind of energy that attracts or repels students.

So to create a culture of high achievement, it begins with the classroom. Make the learning environment reflective of three things:

- The *students* you're teaching
- The *content* you're teaching
- The *values* you're teaching

Most teachers have content information in their classrooms. If they teach math, there are math facts on the wall. If they teach language arts, there are punctuation tips and the eight parts of speech on the wall. This is fine and to be expected, but the first thing needed to create culture of high achievement in your classroom is images of people who look like your students, doing what you want your students to do, being what you want your students to be. In addition, there must be a constant reinforcement of the values you expect your student to operate with.

Those who teach Black children must create opportunities for them to associate excellence in math, science, and other disciplines with Blackness. This can be done, in large part, through the images they see on a daily basis in the classroom and school. What they see in the media often helps them associate ignorance, poverty, drug abuse, and crime with Blackness. In Lisa Delpit's book *Multiplication is for White People*, she quotes a Black student who asked her, "why you trying to teach me to multiply, Ms. Lisa? Black people don't multiply, Black people just add and subtract" (Delpit, 2012). This is what children will think until we show them that mathematical and scientific excellence are an integral part of their ancestral lineage.

I'll never forget eagerly walking with anticipation into a school in the north where 60% of the student population was black and 40% was Latino. I was there to do a presentation to the students in the morning, a Teacher Transformation seminar for teachers in the afternoon, and a *ParentPower!* presentation for parents in the evening. On the walls of the school and classrooms I saw nothing that even remotely gave an indication of the students who populated the school. Adding further insult to injury, this school that had been labeled a school in crisis had adopted a scripted curriculum based on the study of European classics. Something as simple as honoring the cultures of the students on the walls of the school had escaped the administration and teachers.

When I presented "The African Origins of Writing & Mathematics" to the entire 7th and 8th grade class, an hour long presentation, the children were deeply engaged. The gentleman who invited me to speak, a county-level academic coach, confided, "Mr. Akua, many of them refuse to go to class or go to class and curse out their teachers. But they were participating and hanging on your every word. These children have never listened to a presentation that long." Bewildered, I replied, "It never occurred to me that they wouldn't listen and participate enthusiastically."

In a Louisiana school where I did this presentation for over 150 high school students, one young man recorded the entire presentation on his phone, tracking me from one side of the stage to the other and even my PowerPoint pictures on the screen. His phone was confiscated by his teacher because of the school's media policy. Understandably, they didn't know if I had consented to being recorded. I respectfully requested that they return the young man's phone and tell him he has my permission to share the video with friends on Facebook, YouTube and Twitter. *Think of all the other things he could have been recording!* That this young Black male was moved by the images he saw and thought enough of what I was saying to record the entire presentation speaks volumes about his thirst for this kind of knowledge.

> I discovered very early in my teaching career that I could not find the images I was looking for at the local teacher's store. I had to create them.

A large part of that entire presentation is showing visual evidence of historical African excellence. I've done this for thousands of school children K-12, and at colleges and universities for undergraduate and graduate students. The pictures and images, along with the narrative of excellence that many of them have never heard is what makes it a transformative experience for all. Images make the difference.

Preparing a classroom, in and of itself is a ritual because it's more than a classroom—it's a class-*womb*! When you subtract the two months for summer break, two weeks for winter break, and two weeks for Thanksgiving, spring break, and President's Day, you are left with nine months. Alfred Powell, author of *Coaching in the Classroom* and *Hip-Hop Hypocrisy: When Lies Sound Like the Truth*, has suggested that the class-womb is where teachers symbolically, after much labor, give birth to their students at the end of the 9-month year. Therefore, just as a woman's womb is sacred, the class-womb must be carefully and consciously constructed to provide the environment that will properly stimulate the growth of the children who will be birthed from it.

I discovered very early in my teaching career that I could not find the images I was looking for at the local teacher's store. I had to pour through *Ebony* magazines, *Black Enterprise*, *Essence*, and the like, to find the images of sharp, educated, successful, stylish, well-dressed African Americans. I would carefully cut out these pictures and place them on poster boards with catchy sayings, then laminate them.

I remember I had cut out a picture of a beautiful, young, Black woman, pasted it on a poster board with the words, "Brothers, please respect the sisters." It was prominently displayed in the classroom and created opportunities for dialogue and discussion. I had a picture of Susan Taylor, the former editor of *Essence* magazine. Next to her picture was a quote from her: "What we focus on is what we're moving toward." I often made reference to this picture and quote when students were on task and when they got off task.

Many of my students came from homes and neighborhood that had a measure of brokenness. As a result, we were always reading about someone who was achieving against the odds. Asante tells us that "Afrocentricity requires a consciousness of victory (Asante, 1988, p. 50-52). Also, stories that we would read, people we would read about, and discussions in class often centered around "restoring our people to their traditional greatness" as the fifth principle of Kwanzaa, Nia (purpose) instructs us to do (Karenga, 1998). So the picture of Hatshepsut, the woman who ruled Kemet (Egypt) for over 20 years as a pharaoh was prominently displayed with her quote, "I have raised up that which was in ruins, I have restored that which was destroyed."

I found a picture of Martin Luther King sitting in the Birmingham jail. I blew it up and wrote the caption, "Some people go to jail for foolishness. Some go to jail fighting for freedom." Then there was a picture of Imhotep's Step Pyramid, the first large building made of stone. I wrote a caption with the picture that said, "Step-by-step, we're rising to the top!"

 Since I taught language arts, I found a glyph of an ancient Kemetic (Egyptian) scribe writing and put the caption, "The art of language, writing and literature had its genesis in Africa." There were all sorts of pictures to be found *once I started looking*: Black men in suits holding a phone, Black women in suits doing business over lunch, Black men as construction workers, Black women as attorneys, Black boys and girls reading, black teens in caps and gowns with diplomas in hand. Pictures of Black writers, poets, activists, leaders, politicians, etc. were all over my walls and a great source of stimulating classroom conversation. Sometimes I did not put a caption on pictures. The picture itself was worth a thousand words.

One picture might be the focal point of a whole lesson, like the legendary picture of Tommy Smith and John Carlos holding up the Black Power fist at the 1968 Olympic Games. When we studied about the Civil Rights Movement and the Black Power Movement, that became a lesson. What are they doing in the picture? Why? Then I would give them a reading selection on the background. We would read together and discuss it. I would ask, "Why would two premiere athletes who had been training for a lifetime to live their dreams at the Olympics give it all up and risk getting their medals stripped to hold a gloved black fist in the air? Would you do it? Why or why not? Do you think it was worth it?" These are the questions we danced in, through classroom discussions, journal entries, and persuasive essays—cognition, comprehension, and consciousness!

Teachers must create the images they want students to see, then create lessons and activities to illuminate the meaning and messages in the images. This is a great way to teach context clues, figurative language, making inferences, and drawing conclusions. But you should not take on this task by yourself. What I also found, is that for students to really bond with the images you share with them in the classroom environment, they must participate in creating it. *No tie-in, no buy-in*. It's as simple as that. Get the students involved in the process. Students will then begin to proudly take ownership of what they have created and the messages in what they have created.

Noting that my students were in need of some of the mother wit and wisdom that many take for granted, I did a

"Words of Wisdom" activity in which my students were given the task of making banners. They had to pick a quote or proverb from a hat. They then had to type up a banner, print it out, piece and paste it together in preparation for it to be laminated. Once laminated it was ready to be displayed. We placed banners all around the school.

I noticed that when my students were walking to or from lunch with another teacher, they would proudly point to their banner and tell their teacher, "I made that." I also noted on more than one occasion, one of my students admonishing another while pointing to one of their banners to reinforce the message.

"Hey man," a boy might say while nudging another who was acting out. "Discipline yourself so others won't have to!"

He would then point to the banner that said the same thing. The other boy would straighten up. Students were taking ownership of what they had created and using it to set expectations and transform behavior.

While hanging up the banners, the counselor noticed and liked what she saw. She approached two of my students who were busy at work in the halls hanging their banner, making sure it was centered and straight.

"Wow. This is great! Who told you to do this?" she asked two girls.

He would then point to the banner that said the same thing. The other boy would straighten up. Students were taking ownership of what they had created and using it to set expectations and transform behavior.

While hanging up the banners, the counselor noticed and liked what she saw. She approached two of my students who were busy at work in the halls hanging their banner, making sure it was centered and straight.

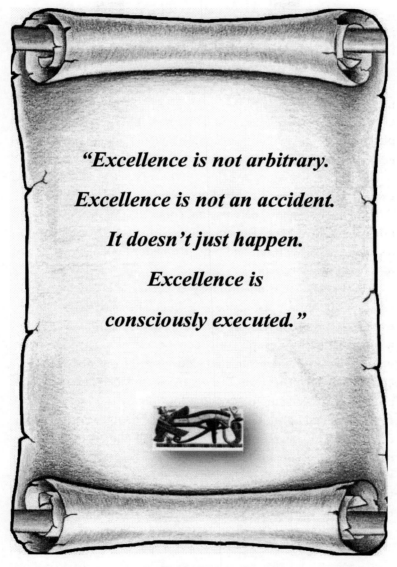

"Excellence is not arbitrary.

Excellence is not an accident.

It doesn't just happen.

Excellence is

consciously executed."

"Wow. This is great! Who told you to do this?" she asked two girls.

"We're in Mr. Akua's class," they responded.

"Where is he?" she asked.

"Just around the corner," they replied.

When the counselor came around the corner and saw more banners being hung, she said, "Mr. Akua, this is great! Is this part of a committee?"

No. It wasn't part of a committee, but part of a *commitment*. "Uncommon accomplishments require uncommon *commitment*." We needn't necessarily start a committee to take on the task of producing excellence. Excellence is the expectation--the specific job of everyone in the building, from the principal, teachers, parents, and counselors to the custodians, and cafeteria workers. But conscious, committed Master Teachers begin with self and radiate transformational energy out to the rest of the school.

Excellence is not arbitrary. Excellence is not an accident. It doesn't just happen. Excellence is consciously executed. I was consciously recreating and operating out of the ancient African philosophy of education, opening the door to the universe for my students to shine like a star. I was also consciously reconstructing Perry's African American philosophy of education: "freedom for literacy and literacy for freedom, racial uplift, citizenship, and leadership" (Perry, Steele, & Hilliard, 2003, p. 10). It was embodied in the banner above my doorway, on the inside and outside of my classroom, which read "Enter to learn, depart to serve." It served as a reminder of the responsibility I wanted my students to accept in making their community "more beautiful and beneficial" (Karenga, 1998).

Questions for Thought, Reflection & Discussion

1. "Uncommon accomplishments requires uncommon commitment." What is the significance of this statement?
2. Describe how teachers can create a climate for transformation in their classroom and school.
3. Explain the power of images to transform and deform consciousness and shape behavior.

Chapter 3:

Education for Identity Restoration

"Identity determines activity."

Several years ago, I was logging in to my email account. On the log-in page was a listing of the days' headlines with a picture in reference to the most important headline of the day. The major news headline read, "Identity theft is the fastest growing crime in America!" The picture was a sinister-looking masked-man holding a laptop computer.

As I travel around the country training teachers and leaders, I always ask the audience to raise their hand if they know someone who was a victim of identity theft. Everywhere I have ever asked this, approximately 70-90% of the audience raises their hand.

I was a victim of identity theft and it was not a pleasant experience. Someone captured my personal information and began using my name and my resources to make unauthorized purchases. Like many others who have been victims of identity theft, I was *confused*, *angry*, and *disillusioned*. It was through this process that what was happening to my students and African American students all over became very clear to me.

In many regards, African American children are victims of cultural identity theft. Someone has stolen their story. Their story has been replaced with a glorified narrative of pimps, playas, criminals, and thugs. And so we have looked on with deep concern at the onslaught of images which gangsterize and criminalize our black male students. We have looked on with the same dismay at the manipulation, objectification, and hyper-sexualization of Black females. I began to realize that the same confusion, anger, and disillusionment that I felt when my identity was stolen, is the confusion, anger, and disillusionment that many black children face today in schools and classroom that are set up to steal their identity and fail them.

The gansterization and criminalization of the culture leads to the dehumanization of the people. This dehumanization then becomes justification for mass extermination through litigation and incarceration. Schools, through their lack of teaching about the best of Black culture become accessories to educational identity theft. In traditional African societies and civilizations, children went to school to remember who they were. Today, many Black children go to school to *forget* (Some, 1997). As a result, in *Too Much Schooling, Too Little Education*, Shujaa notes "schooling is a process intended to perpetuate and maintain the society's existing power relations and the institutional structures that support those arrangements" (Shujaa, 1994, p. 15).

"Education is identity restoration."

For teachers wishing to reach and teach African American students, education is identity restoration. Your class must be geared toward transforming the images of black males and females and consciously creating a culture of high achievement. Theresa Perry argues that "the task of achievement is fundamentally shaped by the very identity of African Americans *as African Americans*" [italics mine] (Perry, Steele, & Hilliard, 2003, p.87). In other words, culture and identity are almost always consciously placed front and center relative to the high achievement of Black children.

Any teacher who wishes to make a critical, transformative impact on African American children must understand what I call "The Pyramid Paradigm for High Performance." It contains the elements which make for the type of education that is consistent with the practices and outstanding results Master Teachers get.

The Pyramid Paradigm for High Performance represents the pathways through which effective instruction must travel for academic and cultural excellence. Every unit, every lesson, every bulletin board, every activity, every project, and every class discussion ought to be created incorporating the overarching principles of the Pyramid Paradigm

The Pyramid Paradigm for High Performance

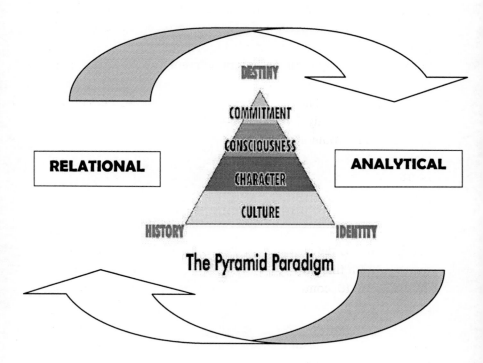

Every lesson, regardless of subject must include African contribution, critique, and consciousness.

At the left base of the pyramid, we see that history comes first. Dr. John Henrik Clarke taught us that, "history is a clock which people use to tell the political an cultural time of day" (Clarke, 1991, p. 25) This suggests that if we do not teach Black children their history, they will not know "what time it is."

Time is of the essence and the dawning of a new day is quickly approaching. Our children are not "at-risk,"—America is; for we can no longer continue to allow the gross mis-education of the masses and multitudes of children.

We know that a tree without roots cannot stand. It is the roots which not only provide physical stability underground for the tree. The roots also provide the vital, life-giving nutrients that allow a tree to live, grow, flourish and bear fruit. The same is true of history and culture, for Clarke also tells us that "a people's relationship to their history is like the relationship of a child to its mother" (Swanson, 2003).

Dr. Runoko Rashidi suggests that "history is the light that illuminates the past and the key that unlocks the door to the future." With this thought in mind, it is no longer necessary for our children to continue to blindly stumble in academic and social darkness.

On the right base of the pyramid, is *identity*. A thorough understanding of our history gives us a vital nutrient which Dr. Edward Robinson calls *Vitamin I* (for identity). As Dr. Na'im Akbar notes in his seminal work *Know Thyself*, "The first function of education is to provide identity" (Akbar, 1999, p. 1). Identity determines *activity*. Currently, we are *Vitamin I* deficient. This suggests that many of our children are suffering from an identity crisis. If our young men think they are n___, they will act like n___. If they think they are thugs, they will act like thugs. If they think they are "pimps and playas,"

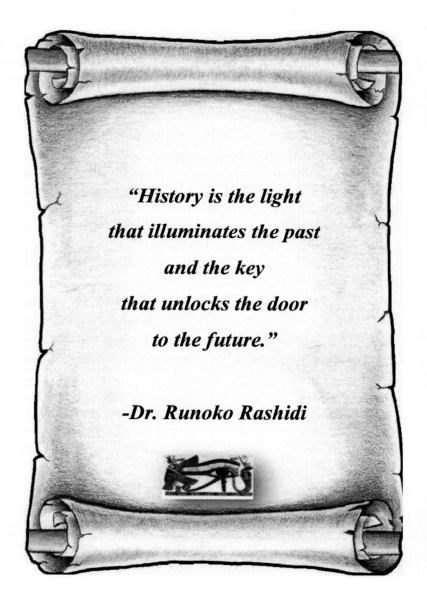

"History is the light
that illuminates the past
and the key
that unlocks the door
to the future."

-Dr. Runoko Rashidi

this is what they will act like, because identity determines *activity*.

Conversely, when our children know that they are the descendents of great masters and builders, they will excel, build strong families, businesses and communities. They will walk with power and majesty, calling forth a new reality, because identity determines activity. Therefore, to know this history and legacy of excellence is not optional, but *essential*. Indeed our children will benefit greatly from this knowledge and insight. The knowledge of this legacy must permeate every discipline. For this to be the case, educators must know the African origins of the discipline they teach.

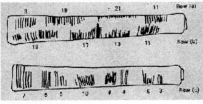

I was once conducting a teacher training and mentioned this point about teaching the African origins of the discipline that you teach. A teacher raised her hand and said that she agreed that our teaching should be culturally relevant, but that the discipline she taught did not have an African origin. "What do you teach?" I asked.

"Math," she replied.

The Ishango Bone was found in 1960 in northeastern Zaire. Upon further examination, the markings on the side were discovered to be, not just arbitrary markings, but mathematical notations denoting

"*The*
first function
of education
is to provide
identity."

-Dr. Na'im Akbar
Know Thyself

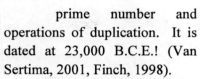

prime number and operations of duplication. It is dated at 23,000 B.C.E.! (Van Sertima, 2001, Finch, 1998).

My wife, quite a master teacher of early childhood education, has also informed me that there is a teaching instrument for elementary math that clearly appears to be inspired by the Ishango Bone.

I then explained to this teacher that the oldest mathematics textbook in the world comes from Africa. The Ahmose mathematics papyrus (often misnomered the Rhind Mathematics Papyrus after the young Scottish attorney who purchased it in the 1800s) is over 3800 years old and known to be a copy of a much older African text, also from Africa. We know this because Ahmose noted this in the papyrus. It contains specific examples of algebra, trigonometry, sine, cosine, tangent, cotangent, area, circumference, volume and much, much more (Obenga, 2004).

Problem #56 from the Ahmose Mathematics Papyrus which details how to find the slope of a pyramid. Source: Finch, Charles (1998):.*The Star of Deep Beginnings: The African Genesis of Science & Technology*.Khenti: Decatur, GA.

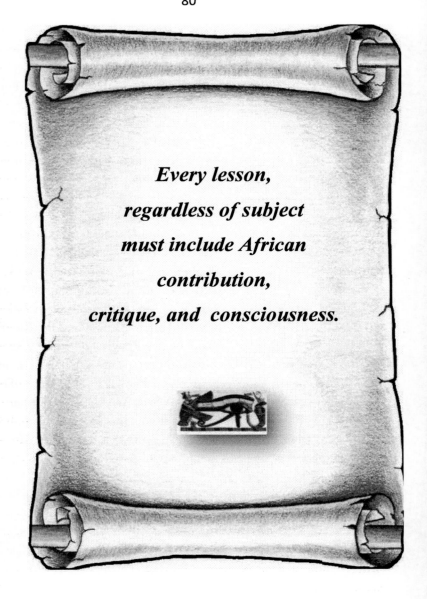

*Every lesson,
regardless of subject
must include African
contribution,
critique, and consciousness.*

Obenga further observes "Electronic calculators in use today have not come up with breakdowns superior to those presented in...the Papyrus Rhind [Ahmose Mathematics Papyrus]" (Obenga, 2004, p. 430). In addition, Ahmose wrote the first written evidence of the scientific method in the preface of the papyrus (Finch, 1998).

Every lesson, regardless of subject must include African contribution, critique, and consciousness. If teachers do not consistently teach the African origin and contribution to the discipline they teach, according to Woodson, "the thought of the inferiority of the Negro is drilled into him in almost every class he enters and in almost every book he studies" (Woodson, 1933, p. 2).

> As an educator seeking personal mastery, I have had to consciously and consistently confront my own miseducation.

Put another way, by default you perpetuate a dynamic of inferiority in black children because it appears and is unconsciously accepted that their people made no contributions to humanity. The absurdity of this is that **the exact opposite is true!** African people have contributed *seminally*, *significantly* , *scientifically*, and tremendously to every discipline of study, bar none. *But teachers cannot teach what they do not know.*

Education for transformation goes beyond contribution. When I suggest that that each lesson include African critique and consciousness, this must include what I will call **African Cultural Inquiry**. This simply means that, in order to facilitate critique and consciousness, we must ask some critical and essential questions. Dr. Marimba Ani suggests that one critical question that can be applied to every grade-level and lesson is,

"Is it good for African people?" We can also add, "What effect will it have on the community? The environment?"

I should also note here that the deep knowledge of African history and culture were not taught to me in my formal schooling. I had to teach them to myself, because I was miseducated. I sought out the works of African scholars who dedicated their lives to "rescuing and reconstructing African history and putting it back into the hands of those who created it" (Karenga, 1998).

Herein lies another essential point worth noting. As an educator seeking personal mastery, I have had to consciously and consistently confront my own miseducation (Woodson, 1933). I had to reconcile the fact that I knew very few details about African contributions to the academic disciplines. So I dedicated myself to the study. It is beyond rewarding. This is part of the task of all educators seeking mastery, especially those teaching African American students.

Just as wise and prudent people supplement their diet with multi-vitamins and other essential nutrients that are not found in many of the foods we eat, it is incumbent upon educators and parents to be sure to supplement the academic diet of our children with the *Vitamin I* that can be found through a careful study of their own culture across all disciplines. In other words, there are African and African American contributions (both ancient and modern) to all subjects and disciplines.

Dr. Asa Hilliard notes, "today, the formal education of most people of African ancestry is usually accomplished in systems that take us far away from ourselves" (Hilliard, 1997). This has led many of our young men and women to assume what Akbar calls, the "alien identity" (Akbar, 1999). This is characterized by self-destructive, counter-cultural, anti-African behavior (including underachievement, apathy,

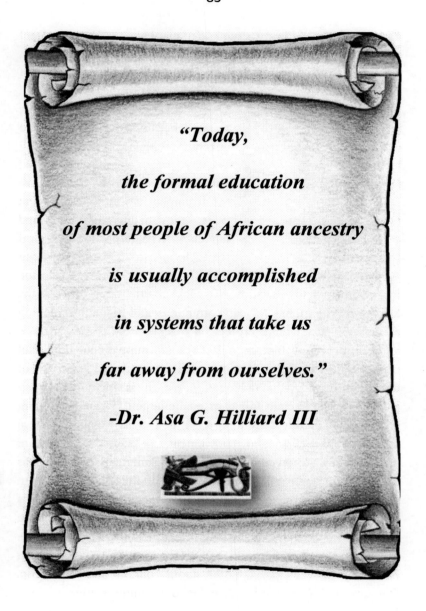

"*Today,*

the formal education

of most people of African ancestry

is usually accomplished

in systems that take us

far away from ourselves."

-Dr. Asa G. Hilliard III

violence, irresponsibility, drug and alcohol abuse, disrespect, and sexual promiscuity, to name a few). The alien identity is a carefully manufactured commodity in service of white supremacy.

> "...create your own personal curriculum of inclusion and curriculum of correction to supplement the school system's prescribed curriculum."

So it is not enough to say, "Your ancestors were kings and queens." Which kings and queens? Where? Under what circumstances? When? What were the triumphs and victories? What were the disappointments and defeats? What are the patterns of the victories and defeats? How can those patterns inform the improvement and elevation of black communities in America along with the global African community and humanity? Doing a Black History Month project on black inventors or writers is good, but certainly not enough. Transformative educators lead their students to the well of ancestral wisdom and the fount of cultural knowledge that they may *daily* drink deeply.

As the ancient father of medicine and pyramid building engineer and architect, Imhotep has much to say to our childen in the way of excellence and achievement. But they can't hear him because they've never heard of him. Ptahhotep has much to teach our children about character. But they can't hear him because they've never heard of him, much less studied his writings. Ahmose, the ancient African writer of the oldest mathematics textbook in history, has much to share about the how math is a reflection of life. Sundiata, the Lion King of Mali has much to teach our children about courage and leadership. But they can't hear him because they don't know who he is.

"Transformative educators
lead their students
to the well of ancestral wisdom
and the fount
of cultural knowledge
that they may
<u>*daily*</u> *drink deeply."*

> When you hear the buzz words, "standards-based," you must ask yourself, "whose standards?"

Dr. Mark Dean led a team of computer scientists who built a microchip which does a *billion* calculations per second. At the ripe age of 35, Dr. Thomas Mensah, a native of Ghana, was one of a few innovative and pioneering engineers who developed the technology that made the cell phone and ATMs possible. Do you think these men, through their accomplishments, might have something to say to our children?

In addition, there needs to be a radical restructuring of the definition of womanhood, lest children continue to be coerced into viewing women as objects of exploitation and pleasure rather than women, worthy of dignity and respect. Mae Jemison, Maxine Waters, Queen Nzingha, Michelle Obama, Queen Tiye, Cathy Hughes and Hatshepsut (and many more) have much to say to our children about what it means to be a woman—and the respect men should accord them.

We can no longer afford to keep the powerful stories of these monumental men and women from our children. In an era of national and state standards, high-stakes testing, minimal competency, scripted curricula, it must be a conscious, thoughtful, and intentional act of determination to create your own personal curriculum of inclusion and curriculum of correction to supplement the school system's prescribed curriculum. This is what black Master Teachers have done for decades, even in the midst of fierce opposition.

When you hear the buzz words, "standards-based," you must ask yourself, "whose standards?" Don't be lulled into thinking that the standards are somehow universal. What are and have been the standards of black Master Teachers through the decades. And what were the standards of ancient African master teachers through the millennia? When you hear "research-driven" or "data-driven," ask yourself, whose research, whose data? Social science research has been used in large measure to justify the status quo.

Ultimately, as Clarke notes, "Education has but one honorable purpose…to prepare the student to be a responsible handler of power. Any other type of education is a waste of time… All education must lead to some type of power…one has to have power in order to be a total human being" (Clarke, 1991, p. 331).

> "Culture is ordered behavior."
> -Dr. Marimba Ani

Educators intent on meeting the needs of African American children must make a calculated effort to constantly and consistently show their students images of excellence, achievement and authentic power that look like them. So many of our children think that crime, violence, incarceration, irresponsible parenting and sexual promiscuity are the norm for Black people. This perception being the case, we must help them *transform the perceived norm* through the positive, life-affirming images we expose them to. In so doing, we will help our children to discern and discriminate between alien self-destructive images and healthy constructive images. It is as if the children are saying, "I can't be what I can't see." Remember, education is *identity restoration*.

But the purpose of studying African culture is not black pride. Black pride is a wonderful and essential by-product of studying the history and the culture. However there is a much deeper reward to be gained in finding answers to the challenges we face because, "…our own cultural traditions provide ample answers to the basic questions that all must ask. We can start from our own African center in the creation of a future. Finally, we can share this humane, democratic, and deeply spiritual way of life with the world" (Hilliard, Williams, & Damali, 1987).

Once our children understand their history and are rooted in their true identity, their future flowers and unfolds into a powerful *destiny*: businessmen, businesswomen, scientists, educators, medical practitioners, engineers, ministers, husbands, fathers, wives and mothers—leaders. Destiny can be defined as our *rightful* place in Eternity—a place of agency and empowerment. However, Eternity must not be viewed as a far off place that we encounter after death. The Ancestors of ancient Kemet (Egypt) taught that, "if we wish to live for Eternity, we must build for Eternity." And when we sow seeds of history, identity, and destiny into our African American children, we awaken within them the urge to leave a *legacy*.

Now we must define the terms inside the Pyramid Paradigm. At the base inside the pyramid is *culture*. Dr. Marimba Ani defines culture as, "ordered behavior" (Ani, 1980). Not ordered behavior in the sense prescribed behavior for the purpose of producing unthinking automatons, but ordered behavior in terms of a set of standards to live by and live up to. We are in the process of restoring order for our children, their families and communities.

Rising up from the base of culture on the Pyramid Paradigm is *character*. An integral part of cultural awareness is character development. We define character as, "the ongoing development of morals, values, critical thinking and decision-making skills." Traditional African systems of education were always infused with character-building activities and lessons. This is why the ancient African writer and philosopher Ankhsheshonqi said, "it is in the development of character that

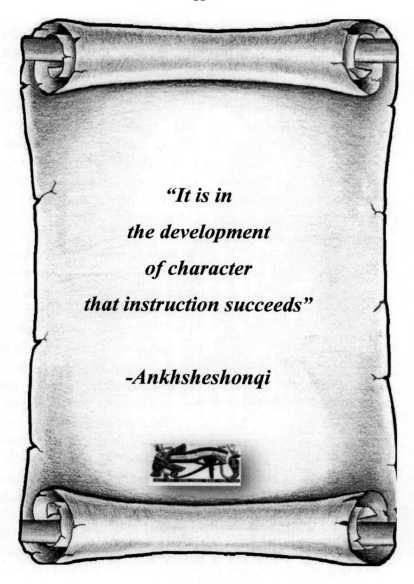

"It is in

the development

of character

that instruction succeeds"

-Ankhsheshonqi

instruction succeeds" (Karenga, 1984). This is why the ancient African educator and writer, Ptahhotep said, "Strive for excellence in all that you do, so that no fault can be found in your character" (Karenga, 1984).

When our children are exposed to proper cultural and character development, a new mental and spiritual phenomenon emerges. We call it *consciousness*. Consciousness is "the expanded awareness of your place in the universe." Our children need their character and their culture to speak to their consciousness. When this happens, they will be transformed by the renewing of their minds.

> African American students are intelligent, creative, energetic, intuitive, inquisitive, and fiercely loyal with a sharp orientation toward social justice.

With this new consciousness comes a new *commitment*—a commitment to actively participate in the resurrection of African people and the redemption of Humanity. Commitment is at the apex of the Pyramid Paradigm because it is the fruits of the culture, character, and consciousness we spoke of earlier.

Enveloping the pyramid is a cycle that is critical to releasing the genius of African American children. It is the understanding that they tend to be relational in their orientation.

Award-winning teacher, administrator and author, Stephen Peters has observed, "Today's students are a tough audience and differ greatly from those of past decades. They bring to school with them a consumer mentality. If they don't find their teachers interesting, they will decide to tune out" (Peters, 2008, p.87). Notwithstanding the truth of the above,

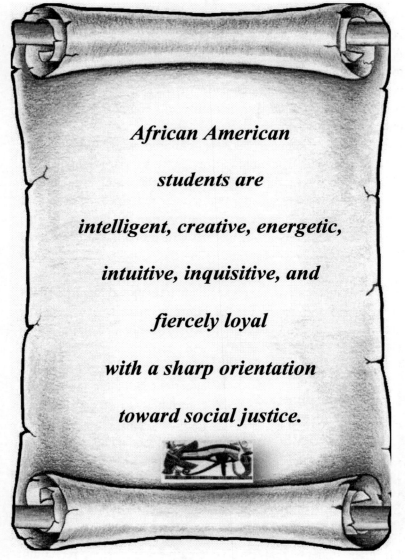

African American

students are

intelligent, creative, energetic,

intuitive, inquisitive, and

fiercely loyal

with a sharp orientation

toward social justice.

African American students are intelligent, creative, energetic, intuitive, inquisitive, and fiercely loyal with a sharp orientation toward social justice.

Educational research has shown that Black children learn best by relating things to their family, environment, experiences, culture, etc. Hale notes:

> The differences between children who function with relational and analytic styles is so great that a child whose cognitive organization is relational is unlikely to be rewarded socially with grades regardless of his native ability, the depth of his information, or his background of experience. In fact, he will probably be considered deviant and disruptive in the analytically oriented learning environment of the school (Hale, 1982, p. 34).

When lessons are presented in a relational manner, Black children are able to master the information much more readily and achieve tremendously. Peters notes further, "...information and subject matter that are disconnected from students' experiences, culture, and needs contribute to their learning problems and ultimately their failure to connect and lack of desire to do so" (Peters, 2008, p. 12).

> When lessons are presented in a relational manner, Black children are able to master the information much more readily and achieve tremendously.

This means Master Teachers must go out of their way to create more activities for their students that involve creative expression, recitation, performance, choral reading, discovery, experimentation, service learning, and freedom of movement (within parameters, of course). So it should be noted here that education for

ℾ ʃ ⋆ ⅄ ɥ

transformation is not just a matter of what is taught (cultural and historical contributions), but *how* it is taught. We will deal with the *how* in the next section.

What we have engaged in here is a brief conversation to illuminate a philosophical foundation. But how do we take these ideas and ideals and turn them into classroom activities and tangible results for Black children? How do we take the great works of Clarke, Hilliard, Akbar, Karenga, Ani, King, Ladson-Billings, Nobles, Wilson, Asante, and others and make the ideas work in the classroom. Let us now move from philosophical foundations to practical classroom applications.

Questions for Thought, Reflection & Discussion

1. What is cultural identity theft? What are its consequences?
2. Examine and share your thoughts on the following quotes:
   - "Education is identity restoration."
   - "The gansterization and criminalization of the culture leads to the dehumanization of the people."
   - African people have contributed *seminally*, *significantly* , *scientifically*, and tremendously to every discipline of study, bar none."
3. Explain the Pyramid Paradigm for Educational Excellence. Give an example of how it might inform lesson planning and delivery of instruction.
4. Explain African Cultural inquiry and the essential questions that are a part of it.

ᚦ ᚲ ✶ ᚴ ᚤ

"*If the Children
don't learn
the way you teach,
teach the way
the Children learn.*"

-Baba Hannibal Afrik

Chapter 4:

The Seba Method (Part I):

Using Rituals to Restoring a Culture of Achievement

From Philosophical Foundation to Practical Application

There are five primary areas that will allow us to actualize the ideas shared in the first part of this book. Employing these application strategies will begin to awaken and release the potential within Black children. In the first part of this book, we discussed curriculum and content. Not only do we find that often the curriculum and content (the *what*) does not adequately serve black children, but the *methodology* (the *how*) employed by teachers does not tap the genius within them.

Sweeping social, cultural and demographic changes in urban schools has caused rapid change in public schools. As a result, most schools of education in the colleges and universities have programs of study that are obsolete and irrelevant by the time the pre-service teacher enters the classroom. However, there are some basic applications that work across the board when thoughtful, caring and committed teachers employ them. I have codified these methods into what I call The Seba Method to help our children shine like a star. The Seba Method is a systematic approach toward setting and building upon a cultural and academic foundation of excellence.

Ritual: a prescribed set of actions that set the stage for a powerful experience.

Student Creed

I am a student seeking to be a scholar.
The standard is excellence, today and tomorrow.
I am disciplined, focused, and on-time.
I am organized, respectful and responsible.
I am on a mission to elevate Myself, my Family,
my Community and Humanity.   Chike Akua ©200

How do you begin class? What are your class rituals? When I coach teachers in my *TeacherTransformation* seminars, this is one of the most powerful lessons relative to creating community in the classroom. Your class rituals determine whether you have a culture of excellence and achievement in your classroom or often, a culture of chaos. By extension, it predetermines the discipline your students will exemplify or the lack of discipline they will demonstrate.

> The words of the Student Creed constituted the *deconstruction* of negative values and the *reconstruction* of positive, life-affirming values.

Prior to employing the power of affirmations, I used to walk into the classroom and say, "Okay, take out your homework/notebook/book…" Students would be talking and sharpening pencils. It often took me five minutes just to get the class settled and on task. This often led to me raising my voice, being frustrated and even losing my voice on many occasions.

But using the Student Creed to begin class ushered in a new way of making my life easier in the classroom. It served as a call to order. It focused my students and called them to task. My policy was that students had to stand up straight, strong, and tall and recite the Creed at the beginning of the class period.

It got to the point where all I had to do was walk into class and say, "I am a student seeking to be a scholar" and students would stand at attention to recite the Creed. Then students began asking if they could lead it. This is where it really got good because now it belonged to them. Pleased with the request (which I fully expected), I would oblige them. They made it their own. The Student Creed became the moral measuring stick when evaluating the behavior of a character in a story and how they handled conflicts. It became something that could constantly be referred to to reinforce the values I expected of my students.

These words of the Creed constituted the *deconstruction* of negative values and the *reconstruction* of positive, life-affirming values. I never asked my students to memorize it. But by reciting it daily, naturally, they did. We took out the key vocabulary words, defined them and discovered their unique meaning within the context of the affirmation.

Oftentimes it was my most challenging boys who wanted to lead the Creed. They craved attention so much. Leading the Creed allowed them to get the attention they craved (which met their emotional needs) and get the leadership experience (which met their academic, social and cultural needs).

When my principal got wind of it, the Student Creed was soon adopted as the *school's* creed. It was read and recited on the announcements every morning. T-shirts with the Student Creed on the back were printed, sold and purchased. Students and teachers would wear these shirts on Fridays. We gradually began to see the climate and the culture of the school change. Fast forward a few years and the Student Creed is now being used in a number of schools across the country. One principal in Chicago even had it painted on a mural in his school's main hallway!

In class, the Student Creed became the foundation we would use to evaluate the behavior of characters in stories and people in history and current events. They now had a cultural and moral *point of reference* to draw from and build upon—a point of reference much more palatable than soft-porn videos, violent and misogynistic music and degenerate talk shows.

Kobie Wilkerson of Love II Learn Educational Group is known for his dynamic and impactful trainings for teachers. In the school he used to teach at, there was a large mirror in the hallway. Everyday when he would walk his students to lunch, they would jump in front of the mirror making silly faces. "Okay," he thought after seeing his students do this day-in and day-out.. "We've got to use this mirror to teach a lesson." Kobie wrote the affirmation for his first graders entitled, "I Love Me!" From that day forward, he and his students performed the affirmation, complete with kinesthetic movements everyday in front of the mirror.

I Love Me!   By L. Kobie Wilkerson

I look in the mirror and what do I see?
I see someone who really likes me!
I work real hard and keep my behavior royal.
I treat others kind and to myself I'll be loyal!
I'm smart and beautiful and have nice words to say,
And there's no one like me and I love this face!
I'm so special because there is no one like me!

I look in the mirror and you know what I see?
I see someone who really loves themself,
And if they could be anyone else in the world they'd be no one else.
You give me a chance to be anyone I could be
And every single time I'd choose me!
I look in the mirror and I'm impressed!
I see someone who does their best!
No matter what may happen, or what may be,
I will always remember how I feel about me!

I LOVE ME! I LOVE ME! I LOVE ME! (Wilkerson, 2008)
Ritual is a prescribed and established set of actions that set the stage for a powerful experience. Using ritual in the classroom, in particular the Student Creed or "I Love Me", does several things:

- It establishes order; it let's students know that class has begun
- It welcomes a spirit of cooperation because the students recite it in unison
- It makes cooperation natural because everyone knows what to do; students will even correct other students who do not immediately snap to attention

Any affirmations that you may choose to use at the beginning of class should serve as a call to order; it must confirm and affirm purpose, values, and goals. Another affirmation that I have used over the years to do this is the rhythmic Transformation Affirmation.

Transformation Affirmation
Love and light, truth and transformation
Healing and harmony, across the nation
Compassion and conviction are the tools for my mission
I open my eyes to see with inner vision
Peace and blessings be unto Humanity
The change begins within; the change begins with me.
Chike Akua ©2001

This affirmation is often done with clapping and a djembe drum if available. Again, we are deconstructing negative values and reconstructing the positive. This affirmation articulates all of the values I want my students to demonstrate.

The spirit and energy that this affirmation conjures up opens the pathway for exceptional learning to take place as we employ kinesthetic techniques of choral reading, body movement, sound and rhythm.

We close class everyday with the Resurrection Affirmation, which gives a charge and reminds us of our unique calling and work in the world.

Resurrection Affirmation
The resurrection of my people and the redemption of Humanity
Depends on whether I accept the call to higher consciousness.
Today, tomorrow, and evermore…I accept the call.

The lesson here is that while we "enter to learn," we "depart to serve."—to serve our family, community and humanity.

Questions for Thought, Reflection & Discussion

1. What is a ritual and what is its function?
2. Explain the power of rituals in the classroom.
3. Reflect upon the following statement: "The words of the Student Creed constituted the *deconstruction* of negative values and the *reconstruction* of positive, life-affirming values."

Chapter 5:

The Seba Method (Part II):

Using Rhythm to Restore a Culture of Achievement

THE SEBA METHOD
Helping students shine like a star

RELATIONSHIP

RITUAL **RHYTHM**

REMEMBRANCE **REPETITION**

Rhythm: "the use of syncopated patterns of sound to enhance students' cognitive functioning, memory and understanding."
A-B-C-D-E-F-G
H-I-J-K-L-M-N-O-P
Q-R-S
T-U-V
W-X-Y-Z

Now I know my ABCs
Next time won't you sing with me.

All schoolchildren in America learn this rhythmic song in preschool or kindergarten. In early childhood education, songs and rhymes are used frequently. For some reason, when children get to middle and high school, this critically effective teaching method is discarded as elementary. Nothing could be further from the truth.

We define rhythm as "the use of syncopated patterns of sound to enhance students' cognitive functioning, memory and understanding." In traditional African societies and centers of learning, rhythm was a foundational element in *everyday life*. It should further be noted that many black children, especially boys are constantly being disciplined for "pencil popping" and creating rhythms with pens on the desks. They are naturally in tune or seeking to get in tune with the rhythm of life. The Master Teacher capitalizes on this and seizes the opportunity to cultivate this into a teaching tool that helps balance the down time when students are expected to sit still and concentrate.

> "Put it to a rhythm and rhyme and you can teach it in half the time."

In teaching my students the eight parts of speech, I wanted to create a rap that would help my students remember the information. What I found out was that the learning of the rap cut my teaching time by more than half and helped them learn to name, define and give examples of the eight parts of speech. Please note that, as a teaching tool, "The Grammar Rap" has each of the eight parts of speech in bold, a definition of each, and examples of each underlined.

Grammar Rap

Good communication skills are essential
The power of the word will make you influential

We need to know the eight parts of speech
Master the language go as high as you can reach.

A **noun** is a person place or thing
An idea in my <u>mind</u> that makes me dream

A **verb** is a word that always shows action
Like <u>divide</u>, <u>multiply</u>, <u>add</u>, and do subtraction.

An **adjective** always describes a noun,
Like a <u>big</u>, <u>red</u> truck you can drive around.

An **adverb** usually ends in –ly.
<u>Clearly</u> a verb is what it modifies

A **pronoun** takes the place of a noun,
Like when <u>she</u>, <u>he</u>, and <u>they</u> walk around.

A **conjunction** connects phrases, clauses and words
<u>And</u>, <u>but</u>, <u>or</u>, <u>nor</u>, and <u>yet</u>—haven't you heard.

Here's a word that's definitely on a mission.
Let me give you some examples of a **preposition**
<u>In</u>, <u>on</u>, <u>from</u>, <u>to</u>, and <u>around</u>,
<u>during</u>, <u>after</u>, <u>up</u> and even <u>down</u>.

Now we need to learn about **interjections,**
A word with enthusiasm, lots of expression!
Like <u>STOP!</u>, <u>GO!</u>, <u>WAIT!</u>, <u>YES!</u>, and <u>NO!</u>
<u>WOW!</u>, <u>GREAT!</u>, <u>AWESOME!</u>, <u>UH-OH!</u>

Now that you know the eight parts of speech,
master the language, go as high as you can reach!
Chike Akua ©2004

It was wonderful to see how my sixth, seventh, and eighth grade students took the words to the rap, changed the beat and rhythm, performed it, then wrote and typed a 10-page grammar handbook, with great proficiency. My wife has used "The Grammar Rap" with her second graders and raved about the results.

In both cases, the students emerged ready to take the lead in rapping the lyrics. I even videotaped their outstanding performances. The power of rhythm can be used with math, ,history, science and language arts facts. Students are innovative and can be encouraged to create their poems, raps, and pneumonic devices to help them better learn and understand content.

Questions for Thought, Reflection & Discussion

1. Why is rhythm an essential part of the process of educating children? Explain.
2. Reflect upon this statement: "Put it to a rhythm and rhyme and you can teach it in half the time."
3. What effective methods and modes of instruction are present in the Grammar Rap? Explain.

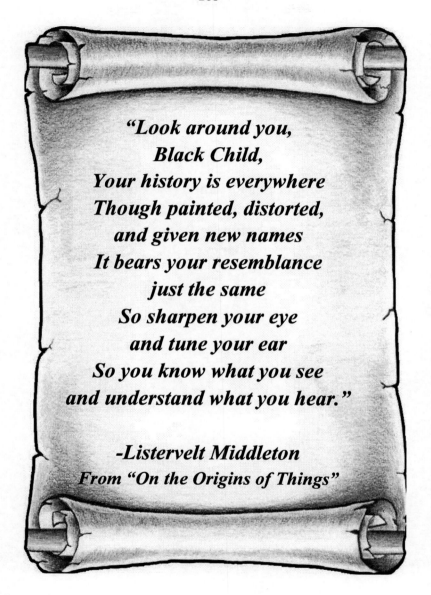

"*Look around you,*
Black Child,
Your history is everywhere
Though painted, distorted,
and given new names
It bears your resemblance
just the same
So sharpen your eye
and tune your ear
So you know what you see
and understand what you hear."

-Listervelt Middleton
From "On the Origins of Things"

Chapter 6:

The Seba Method (Part III):

Using Remembrance to Restore a Culture of
Achievement

𓏺 𓋴 ⋆ 𓃡 𓀁

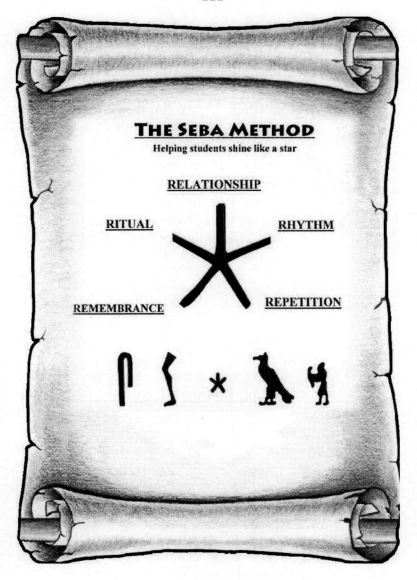

THE SEBA METHOD
Helping students shine like a star

RELATIONSHIP

RITUAL   RHYTHM

REMEMBRANCE   REPETITION

Remembrance is an evolving awareness of the contributions of Africa and her people throughout the world. It is embodied in

the west African concept of *sankofa*. Sankofa means, "return and retrieve it" (Karenga, 1998). It is the perennial quest to retrieve one's history, culture, and legacy and remain grounded in it. It is represented by the mythical sankofa bird which turns its head all the way around to look behind itself. This concept is further illuminated in the African proverb which says, "to go back to the past is the first step forward."

However, there are three critical mistakes that many teachers make consistently relative to teaching about the contributions of African people to humanity:

1. They relegate such teaching to February, the shortest month of the year.
2. They begin the story of African people with the period of enslavement or civil rights, leaving out thousands of years of independent African excellence and achievement.
3. They relegate the teaching of African contributions to the social studies/civics/history class.

As a result, many Black children have *cultural amnesia*. Of course, amnesia is a severe loss of memory. This loss of cultural memory is what has allowed others to supplant African identity with a self-destructive, alien identity. The alien identity becomes a cancer spreading throughout the community.

> "…we can increase reading comprehension and cultural consciousness at the same time."

When someone has lost part of their memory, there are basic steps that are taken to resuscitate the memory. They are shown pictures of great moments from their past. They are told wonderful stories about themselves and their family members. Herein lies the key to remembering a dismembered mind. We must take the responsibility for putting the consciousness back together again.

In facilitating the journey to cultural consciousness, it is critical that teachers use materials produced by conscious Africans, those grounded in the African-centered perspective. Often the story of African people, their culture and their history either gets told incorrectly or doesn't get told at all. I highly recommend the curriculum resources of Anthony Browder and Molefi Asante. While both of these outstanding scholars are known for their scholarly books for adults, they also have cutting-edge reading materials for children and adolescents—books grounded in an authentic African worldview. In addition, my work has been dedicated to building a bridge between African-centered scholars and practical classroom reading resources and activities.

It should also be noted that the African-centered worldview is not a worldview that promotes hate. There have been many misrepresentations of what the African-centered perspective is about. It "does not seek to deny or deform others' history and humanity, but to affirm, rescue, and reconstruct its own" (Karenga, 1998, p. 52). Additionally, "truthful, equitable, and culturally appropriate education is understood to be a basic human right" (King, 2005, p. *xxiii*).

> "Often the story of African people, their culture and their history either gets told incorrectly or doesn't get told at all."

Knowing the critical nature and need for this type of culture-centered knowledge (King, 1995) to get to our children I asked long time friend, colleague, and former Teacher of the Year, Tavares Stephens to co-author *Reading Revolution: Reconnecting the Roots*. It is a collection of ninety reading selections set up in the standardized testing format. The reading selection is on the left column and ten multiple choice questions on the right.

Our premise was that we can raise comprehension and cultural consciousness at the same time. When this resource was introduced to other teachers, they clamored to get copies to share with their students because they knew of no other resource like it. Dr. Vonzia Phillips, director of Premier Middle Schools for Dekalb County Schools (Atlanta) in Georgia, remarked, "At a time when teachers across the nation are struggling to find that delicate balance between curricular standards and meaningful content that students will readily identify with, Mr. Akua and Mr. Stephens have definitely hit the mark with *Reading Revolution*."

Many teachers have remarked that *Reading Revolution* opened up incredible and insightful dialogue with students on critical issues and inspired their students to strive for excellence. Simultaneously, it increases their understanding and achievement. We suggest to teachers and parents that their child read one selection per day. This is their daily cultural multi-vitamin. It is the least that our children should be learning about where they come from.

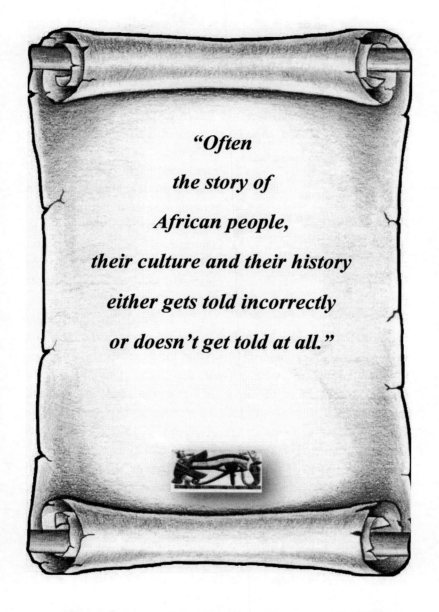

"*Often*

the story of

African people,

their culture and their history

either gets told incorrectly

or doesn't get told at all."

Just as a person who takes a vitamin still eats other foods to get nutrients and nourishment, Black boys still need to be exposed to as much of their history and culture as possible.

Co-author, Tavares Stephens remarks, "*Reading Revolution* is not the first book of its kind. Other biographies covering people of African and African American descent have been written. Yet *Reading Revolution* possesses unique applications. It is an interdisciplinary text aimed at enhancing test-taking and critical thinking skills while lifting the mind and spirit through inspirational selections. This text will break cycles of underachievement" (Akua & Stephens, 2006).

> Another striking result of using ***Reading Revolution*** is that students began to demonstrate increased interest in class.

I used this curriculum resource with a group of students who did not pass the state test in reading and language arts. After affirmations, class began with 10 minutes of silence (with soft music playing: jazz or classical) for them to read the selection and answer the questions. Then we would take 10 minutes to read the selection orally, analyze and answer the questions. The rest of the class period was spent on other activities.

We showed these students the structure of the test and how to look for and identify topic, main idea, supporting details, and context clues. We taught them, "don't fall for the trick that the test-maker tries to play on you, the test-taker." It then became almost like a game to see who wouldn't get tricked. So they began to notice the patterns of common mistakes that are made. *None* of these students had passed the state test the previous year, yet 72% of them passed after going through *only half* of the *Reading Revolution* exercises.

> We taught them, "don't fall for the trick that the test-maker tries to play on you, the test-taker."

Another striking result of using these reading selections is that students began to exhibit increased interest in class. They began to look forward to their daily reading selection. They would see me in the hallway or at my door and ask, "Who are we reading about today, Mr. Akua?" One day during the last period, a young man came to class and asked with a sigh, "Mr. Akua, can't we just chill today?" I had always told my students that class wasn't the place to chill. They could "chill" at home. Nonetheless, he asked anyway.

With a smile, I replied, "You know you've been waiting all day just to see who we're going to read about today!" His response astounded me. "Yeah," he shrugged his shoulders, "you're right." He sat down, got out his pen and got ready to read. We are currently in the process of producing *Reading Revolution* as supplemental, interactive software that will continue to help increase and improve reading comprehension and cultural awareness.

Kortni Boyd is an elementary educator with 10 years of experience. Between teaching and tutoring, she works with 10-14 year olds. "My young scholars fell in love with *Reading Revolution*, she says. The reading passages and comprehension questions are challenging and age appropriate. A number of our young scholars lack understanding and insight as to who they really are. They do not understand that they come from greatness, and rich knowledge, creativity, and wisdom. *Reading*

Revolution was a much-needed blessing to my classroom and my scholars. It truly opened their eyes."

View a sample reading selection of George Washington Carver from *Reading Revolution* below:

‖◆‖‖‖◆‖‖‖◆‖‖‖◆‖‖‖◆‖‖‖◆ 25 ◆‖‖‖◆‖‖‖◆‖‖‖◆‖‖‖◆‖‖‖◆‖‖‖

Ahmed Baba and the University of Sankore

From the 1300s to the 1700s, Timbuktu was one of the greatest cities in all of Africa. Situated near the Niger River, this great center of learning was known throughout the land. It was also an important trading center for gold, salt, iron, and books. Timbuktu had quite a reputation for educational excellence and wealth—so much so, that students and scholars came from all over Africa, Asia , and Europe to study at the famed University of Sankore. Being near the river gave people easy access to this thriving city of trade and education and attracted many people.

Ahmed Baba was the President of the University of Sankore for 30 years. During this time he upheld the African standard of excellence, running the university with great vision. Also during this time, he authored 42 books. This means he wrote more than one book per year in addition to his duties as president. Additionally, Ahmed Baba had over 1600 books that he owned in his personal library. This shows that he knew the power of books to transform the mind. To Africans who introduced the art of writing to the world, books were sacred and holy.

Books were valued so much that people paid for books using only gold. The book a person desired to purchase would be placed on one side of a scale and gold dust would be sprinkled on the other side of the scale until the scales were balanced. Books in Timbuktu and in the Empires of Mali and Songhay were literally, "worth their weight in gold." Because of this, the book industry was just as lucrative as the gold, salt, and iron industries.

People who studied at Timbuktu learned law, medicine and healing, writing and literature, astronomy (study of the stars), and agriculture (the study of farming) and much more. They took their knowledge and understanding of what they learned back to other parts of Africa, Asia, and Europe. Some even came to America. History also shows us that virtually every home in Timbuktu had an extensive library of books and manuscripts.

A portrait of Ahmed Baba (right) and the University of Sankore at Timbuktu (below).

1. The word *situated* means:
   a. educated
   b. dictated
   c. located
   d. truncated
2. People came from _____ to attend the University of Sankore:
   a. all over Africa
   b. Europe
   c. Asia
   d. all of these
3. What attracted people to Timbuktu?
   a. the University of Sankore
   b. the trade industry
   c. the fact that it was near the river
   d. all of these
4. Which of the following *best* proves that Ahmed Baba was an effective educational leader at University of Sankore?
   a. he remained president for 30 years
   b. he knew how to read
   c. he had 1600 books in his personal library
   d. he actually wasn't an effective leader
5. Ahmed Baba knew that books:
   a. were not very important
   b. could transform a person's mind
   c. could not be written by Black people
   d. a and c only
6. The word *lucrative* means:
   a. profitable
   b. poor
   c. pitiful
   d. penitent
7. The word *sacred* means:
   a. ungodly
   b. holy
   c. devilish
   d. church
8. What evidence shows the value of books in Timbuktu?
   a. books were paid for using gold dust
   b. almost every home had a library
   c. people made as much money with books as with gold, salt, and iron
   d. all of these
9. People who studied at University of Sankore:
   a. took the information back to Asia, Europe, and all over Africa
   b. were poor students
   c. didn't take their studies seriously
   d. none of these
10. Which of the following was offered at University of Sankore?
   a. agriculture and astronomy
   b. medicine and healing
   c. writing and literature
   d. all of these

Reading Revolution   ©2006 Chike Akua & Tavares Stephens

⌐ ∫ ★ ⅄ ⅌

A Treasure Within: Stories of Remembrance & Rediscovery is a book of three short stories in which young people encounter ancient ancestors to learn about traditional morals, values, culture, and history. I developed the characters and conflicts based on characteristics of my middle school students and their experiences. Though I was writing for middle and high school students, it has gained a great deal of popularity among elementary students and teachers. There is also the *Parent/Teacher Resource Guide* which is a complete companion curriculum to the three short stoies in *A Treasure Within*.

Hilliard states:

> *A Treasure Within* is the book that many of us have been waiting for. The deep thinking of Ancient Africa is grasped and clearly communicated through these three powerful stories.
>
> Families, counselors, teachers, students, and the community, in general, can relate directly to these stories. Akua blends his keen perceptions of youth culture and their issues with an authentic African World View, demonstrating its application to the   here and now.
>
> It is the writers, artists, dancers, musicians, actors, and playwrights, who have always had the power to transmit our deep culture to the masses. It is also our spiritual leaders who have the obligation to be true to our culture. I am thankful for this outstanding contribution to our mental and spiritual liberation. Our ancestors are pleased. Amun is satisfied (Akua, 2001).

Language arts teacher, Marlena Alvarado observes, "The magic of these stories is not merely the colorful characters that come alive, but the principles of a moral life that foster a strong and beautiful spirit. These stories reach beyond the lines of ethnicity and touch the center of the soul. Atlanta parent, Jackie Miles states, "The principles woven into *A Treasure Within* provides strength and encouragement in an area of urgent need— the moral development of our children."

Ten-year middle school teaching veteran, Anthony Outler says, "I teach social studies, reading, and language arts. I have been using *A Treasure Within* since 2001 and it has been transformative for the students that I teach. It is a powerful tool. They get captivated by the stories."

Brandon Lewis is the founder of the S.T.E.P. Program. It stands for Stepping Towards Educational Progress. We've used *A Treasure Within* every year to transform the lives of third through fifth graders. This book increased academic achievement, improved character development and cultural awareness. His students Daniel says, "I am thirteen years old. I read *A Treasure Within* when I was eleven. Before reading, I would get into fights over stupid things and say hurtful things to my friends, but now that I've read this book, I can calm myself down and be a good sport." Jacqueline, another S.T.E.P. Program student is thirteen and read *A Treasure Within* when she was twelve. She says, "This book changed my life a lot. When I was in elementary school, I was a hot-head. I had a short temper and I would get mad over the littlest things. But now, after reading *A Treasure Within*, I am one of the calmest people ever and I stay away from drama."

Philadelphia parent, Danyeal Sellers observes, "When I read *A Treasure Within* with my children, I felt strongly that this is a book every child, parent,   and teacher should read. It is packed with cultural   and   historical wisdom--the kind of wisdom we   should be sharing with our students every day to light and guide their path."

ſ ⸱ ⋆ ⸱

Sellers felt so strongly that she organized Khepera Charter School's Bennu Dancers & Drummers to dramatize the first story in the book. In 2011, she produced the full-scale production, attended by hundreds of parents, students, educators, community, social, and civic leaders at Philadelphia's Independence Seaport Museum and Concert Hall. By all accounts, it was phenomenal. Her goal is to produce full-scale productions of the remaining two stories in *A Treasure Within* also.

In the first two stories the main characters travel back in time to ancient Kemet (Egypt). After completing these stories with a group of seventh graders, our culminating activity was to take ancient Kemetic symbols and do a project. I knew the project would have powerful results, however, even I was shocked at how tremendous the response was from the students.

Their assignment was to choose from a list of symbols I gave them. They were to type a one-page essay detailing what the symbol meant in ancient times and what it means *to them* today. This stimulates the affective domain. Lastly, they had to purchase a fiberglass ceiling tile and carefully, colorfully, and creatively paint the symbol on the ceiling tile. "Those tiles that meet the standard of excellence will be placed in the ceiling of the main entrance to the school. Our Ancestors left clear examples of excellence and achievement. We will do the same. Your projects will remain in the ceiling for years to come, long after you leave this school," I explained.

James (7th grade) writes:

"I'm doing my project on the symbol the scarab. It is a symbol of transformation which many of us are going through at this time in our lives. I thought it would be interesting to study something that is happening in my life and I really wanted to know the meaning of it.

The scarab lays its eggs in a ball of dung and pushes it in the direct path of the sun until the eggs hatch. Why is this important to me? Even if you're not from a good household and there is crime and your family is poor, it doesn't matter. You can walk in the direct path of the sun. You can transform and be whatever you want to be. You are always in the direct path of the sun and you can transform (change) at any time."

Lindsay (7th Grade) writes:

"The ankh is a symbol of everlasting life related to the female because the female is entrusted with the responsibility to bring forth new life into the world. It is important to me because it represents my gender and shows appreciation to my mother who gave me life. She instills in me each day the importance of who and what I should be. It is so very important to me because I have seen my mother being a strong woman over the past year. She has fought two rounds of breast cancer, but she is always determined not to let it hinder her daily life. She is the "ankh" of my life."

IIIIXIIIIXII www.MyTeacherTransformation.com IIXIIIIXIIII

Ezekiel (7th grade) writes:

"I chose the symbol of the Third Eye because it represents the ability to see and gain insight with more than just the two physical eyes. After reading Mr. Akua's book (A Treasure Within) about Marcus and Imani, it has shown me how difficult it is to open my Third Eye. It takes a focused mind to reach success in life and the Third Eye will show you the way. I also chose this symbol because it happens to be the one that interests me the most.

The Third Eye is also called "the eye of all-seeing enlightenment" for mental and spiritual vision. To me the Third Eye is like the North Star because it leads you in the right direction when you are lost.

The Third Eye is important to me because it will keep you from going in the wrong direction. It is like a compass that leads you where you want to go. These things are important in life because I want to be successful."

Latisa (7th Grade) writes:

"I have chosen the pyramid as my Kemetic symbol. I chose this symbol because it deals with your every day life. Every day of your life you have to stay spiritually, mentally, emotionally, and physically fit. You have to prepare yourself before you step out into the world. If you don't have yourself together, then you won't be able to make it. The pyramid symbolizes the four dimensions of the nature of man and woman: spiritual, mental, emotional, and physical. There are four sides to the pyramid which represent the four parts of woman and man."

James, Lindsay, Ezekiel, and Latisa were in my language arts class. My reading class read the third story in *A Treasure Within*, which was entitled "Daniel & the Djembe Drum." This is a story about a 13 year old boy named Daniel who is coming of age, dealing with peer pressure and the untimely death of his father when he was four years old. A Ghanaian elder teaches Daniel the ancient art of drumming and leads him to a transformational encounter. Since Daniel's drumming instructor is from Ghana, I introduced the students to the Adinkra symbols of Ghana.

Students were given a list of Adinkra symbols and their meanings (instead of Kemetic symbols) to choose from for their final project. Alfred writes:

"The Adinkra symbol I chose was Nkruma Kesee, which in Twi means, "greatness." Adinkra symbols were first used by the Akan, Gyaman, and Ashanti people. All the Adinkra symbols are in the language of Twi of the Akan people.

To me, Nkruma Kesee means more than just the word greatness. It means that everyone, even if you are the poorest person, can do many great things if you put your mind to it. The reason I chose this symbol is because this symbol really makes me feel that I can be great anytime and anywhere. The greatness that I want to achieve is to one day become President of the United States. To me this symbol can show people what greatness really is."

Lincoln chose the same symbol, but had a slightly different take on greatness. He writes:

"The symbol I chose for my project is Nkruma Kesee: greatness. This symbol means a lot to me because I try to achieve greatness in everything I do. I chose this symbol because its circle has no starting or ending point.

The dictionary meaning of greatness is, 'very large, larger in size than others of the same kind, remarkable or outstanding in magnitude, degree or extent; of outstanding significance or importance, chief or principal, superior in quality or character; noble, grand, aristocratic, and enthusiastic.'

This symbol is important to me because it is so powerful. Not everyone can be put on the level of greatness. People are too quick to put themselves on the higher level. You cannot be great in a short time. I feel you must continually do good things to have greatness. Greatness is a mark you are left with when you earn it. You can look at some sports stars, authors, and other people to see greatness in many ways. Greatness is something that everyone can accomplish in their lifetime if they try. Greatness is within all of us..."

These essays represent just a taste of what the children came up with, not to mention the incredible artwork they did with their ceiling tiles. Their tiles were displayed in the main hall of the school and remain there to this day. When I moved to another school and came back to visit, the security guard said, "Mr. Akua, I meant to tell you something. Whenever parents come to visit the school the first thing they see and mention is how incredible those ceiling tiles look."

Questions for Thought, Reflection & Discussion

1. Comment on the three critical mistakes that are often made relative to the teaching of Black history.
2. Reflect and comment on the following statement: "Often the story of African people, their culture and their history either gets told incorrectly or doesn't get told at all."
3. Which of the student essays written about Kemetic and Adinkra symbols stands out to you? Explain why.

Chapter 7

The Seba Method (Part IV):

Using Repetition for Reinforcement

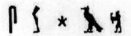

THE SEBA METHOD
Helping students shine like a star

RELATIONSHIP

RITUAL

RHYTHM

REMEMBRANCE

REPETITION

Repetition: The *meaningful* repeating of rituals, activities, lessons, and strategies to guide students toward mastery and achievement.

In repeating the successful strategies of Ritual, Rhythm, and Remembrance, teachers will find that students adopt and adapt a higher level of consistency and proficiency in their work. They show more interest, respect, and responsibility. In addition, these strategies transform a classroom into "a Temple of Higher Learning." These strategies change a school year into a rites of passage. Children entered at the beginning of the year as students. They emerged at the end of the year as scholars. Put simply, it gets results.

It should be stated from the outset, that repetition does not refer to "drill and kill," but meaningfully going over rituals, activities and lessons to reinforce the skills, views, and values, we want black children to internalize and express. "Drill and kill" is usually done in preparation for high-stakes, standardized tests. This kind of instruction, in which everything hinges on test results, often kills the spirit of the students. They often know intuitively that another agenda, other than true education, is at hand.

This is not to suggest that testing be banished. It is, however, to suggest that testing be put in proper place and perspective.

Beginning class everyday with the Student Creed or some sort of pledge that affirms commitment to excellence is an example of repetition. Using a selection from *Reading Revolution* everyday in class is an example of repetition. Choosing a captain or line leader to guide the class through the halls to the cafeteria or media center is yet another.

Atlanta-area principal, Patrick Muhammad understands the power of repetition in conjunction with technology. He

ſ ʃ ⋆ ʌ ʧ

Tweets the SAT word of the day to his *elementary* students and parents. This sets the expectation of college readiness and success very early.

It is through repetition that cooperation becomes natural as Nobles' definition of culture explains. It is through repetition that "ordered behavior" is expressed as in Ani's definition of culture. This repetition creates and further maintains the culture of high achievement that we seek.

Even when there is a breakdown in the normal go of things, repetition restores Ma'at (order), even in the absence of authority. A case in point is exemplified in my ninth year of teaching. I was burning the candle at both ends. My first son was born. I was in graduate school and teaching full-time. In addition, I had been working diligently to finish writing *A Treasure Within*. Sleep was a valuable commodity in short supply. As a result, my health was severely compromised and I kept losing my voice to sinus problems.

One day, barely able to keep my head up with all the congestion in my nose and throat, I met my 7th period class at the door. That year, I was in a trailer. I had brought my djembe drum to school and I would sit on the small deck and play as my students came into the trailer from the main school building. The students enjoyed this and the repetition of this ritual paid tremendous pedagogical dividends.

When I met my 7th period class at the door, I pulled one of my students, Brittany, aside to let her know that I had no voice, needed her to do the Student Creed, and give the class instructions on the activity of the day. This she did and the class settled into the activity in good time and order. And it's a good thing they did because I was completely exhausted.

That year, because we were in a trailer, I not only began class with drumming, I would often conclude class with a drum roll and a brief rhythm. As it was time to get students ready to board the buses, I pulled my drum close, tilted it back, placed it between my knees, and began a drum roll. Students looked up abruptly. They had been so focused on their work, they had forgotten what time it was. Because I wasn't feeling well, I was acutely aware of the time. When students heard the rhythm, Brittany stood up and said, "Come on y'all, Mr. Akua is tellin' us to get ready to get on the bus." The students looked over at me. I smiled, unable to say a word. They began closing books and notebooks and collecting papers. Brittany led the class in our closing affirmation, the Resurrection Affirmation. Then students sat quietly waiting for their buses to be called over the intercom.

This type of cooperation doesn't just happen. It was the result of several months of repeating rituals, lessons, and activities that stimulated my students and let them know what the expectation was. So excellence and achievement is not a one-shot deal. It is systematic, structured, and sophisticated. But it is also relatively simple when clear steps are followed. Repetition reinforces all that we want our children to know.

Questions for Thought, Reflection & Discussion

1. For the purposes of Education for Transformation, what is repetition?
2. Describe the difference between repetition and "drill and kill."
3. How should you as the teacher determine what is to be repeated?

Chapter 8:

The Seba Method (Part V):

Using Relationships to Restore a Culture of Achievement

Ritual, rhythm, and remembrance are powerful methods of what Hilliard calls "purposeful transformation" (Hilliard, 1997). However, none of these strategies work if you as a teacher do not go out of your way to establish a caring *relationship* with students based on belief in their abilities, love, and high expectations. *Everything hinges on relationship.* That's why Relationship is at the top of the Seba Method diagram. It is one thing to teach subject-matter and information, quite another to teach *children.* Students know intuitively whether you want to be there teaching. They know whether you like children, whether you care about them and believe in them. They internalize all of these intuitions.

> It is one thing to teach subject-matter and information, quite another to teach *children.*

I have found that students who resisted behavioral modification or academic instruction from other teachers they did not know or care for, exhibited a willingness to modify their behavior and improve academically because of their *relationship* to me. I have received testimony from hundreds of other teachers affirming this fact. Students who know that you care and who respect your teaching methods will perform for you. They will perform out of a sense of responsibility and fidelity.

It has been said that "rules without relationship equals rebellion." When you have a caring relationship with a student, they will often go the extra mile. They don't go the extra mile because they are necessarily mature enough and understand the long-term benefits. They go the extra mile for the teacher that they love and that loves them.

There are **Ten Nonverbal Questions** I believe students intuitively ask their teachers:

1. Do you care about me?
2. What do you know about me?
3. What do you know about where I'm from?
4. Do you know what is important to me?
5. Do you know what I deal with on a day-to-day basis?
6. Do you know my learning style?
7. What do you like and appreciate about me?
8. Who do you think I am?
9. What do you think I will become?
10. Do you want to be here teaching me?

> When you have a caring relationship with a student, they will often go the extra mile.

The teachers' answers to these questions are found in the way they interact with their students, how they speak to them, how they structure their classroom, lessons, and instruction. If students do not feel the right answers from their teacher(s) regarding these questions, they tend to disengage. Journal writing and sharing is a great way to learn more about your students. Remember, African American students tend to have a relational orientation.

The journal questions I would ask my students to respond to always gave me insight into who they were and what was important to them. Their entries had to be a "well-developed paragraph." This meant five to seven well-developed sentences (or three to five sentences for some of my more reluctant writers). The idea was for them to paint a picture in my mind with rich, descriptive words.

The journal question might ask them to respond to yesterday's lesson or a current event. Monday's journal question was always, "Explain what you did over the weekend. Friday's journal question was always, "Explain the Quote of the Week," a powerful quote or proverb which was always written at the top of the board.

> Journal writing and sharing is a great way to learn more about your students.

Journal writing and journal entry sharing gives students the opportunity to be heard. Often, students are talked *at* and talked *to*. African American students are very expressive and have much to share when given the opportunity in a safe, encouraging, and supportive classroom environment. Your relationship with students should be firm, fair, friendly, and faithful. It should be firm in the sense that excellence is the only option. If you give children an opportunity to be less than excellent, then they will. The standard is excellence and the teacher provides an accessible pathway for the child to meet the standard.

Your relationship with students should be fair. Some students require more time and attention than others. Some students even require a different set of rewards and consequences. So the distribution of time, attention, and rewards may not be equal, but they must be fair according to what each child's needs are. Children have an acute sense of justice; they are quick to point out when something is unfair. Many will rebel or just shut down in the face of unjust classroom practices. Determine top be fair in all your dealings with students.

Lastly, be friendly. While the root word of friendly is friend, I am not suggesting here that you should be a friend to students. This can become very problematic because it sends mixed messages about authority

ﾉ ﾟ ＊ ﾞ

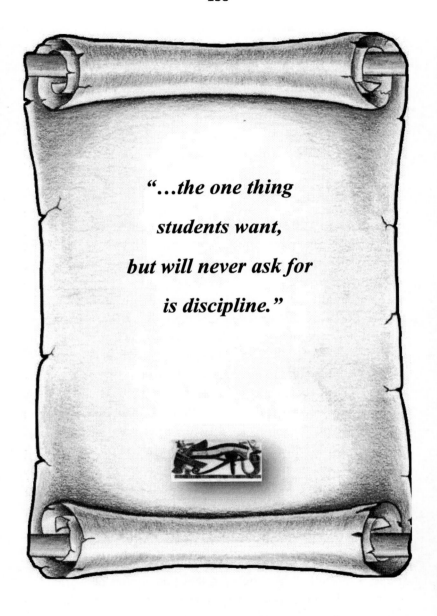

"...the one thing students want, but will never ask for is discipline."

Old school teachers used to suggest, "don't crack a smile 'till May." However, students today need to see teachers engaging them with warm and caring attitudes while maintaining high expectations and clear, direct instructions.

> "...children crave love, attention, fun, and a challenge if they have been properly equipped to meet the challenge."

Teachers who try to be a friend to students often find the lines between adult and child, teacher and student, blurred. Delpit notes, "Black children expect an authority figure to act with authority. When the teacher instead acts as a 'chum,' the message sent is that this adult has no authority, and the children react accordingly" (Delpit, 1995, p. 35).

I have noticed that the one thing students want, but will rarely ask for is *discipline*. Children do not like to be in disorganized and unstructured environments. While there may be initial disenchantment with structure and discipline, students come to expect it and enjoy it.

As a matter of fact, when students are then turned loose in an unstructured, undisciplined environment, they will demand a properly structured and disciplined environment. The only thing worse than never being exposed to a Master Teacher, is having a Master Teacher, then being sent the next year or next semester to a mediocre teacher.

In addition to discipline, children crave love, attention, fun, and a challenge if they have been properly equipped to meet the

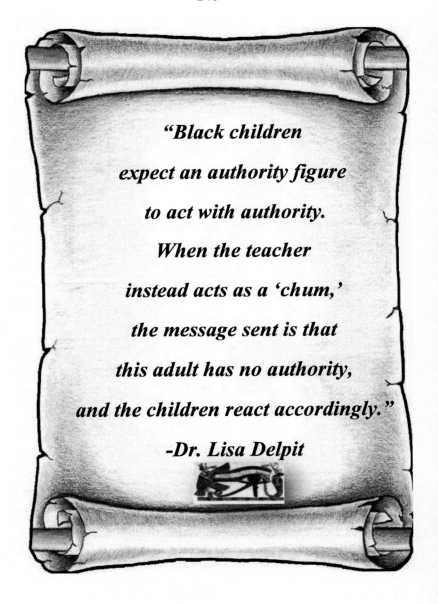

"*Black children*

expect an authority figure

to act with authority.

When the teacher

instead acts as a 'chum,'

the message sent is that

this adult has no authority,

and the children react accordingly."

-Dr. Lisa Delpit

challenge. Teachers who provide these things in a nurturing, affirming environment while using relational, culturally conscious methods tend to be very successful in helping children achieve.

> All the students in my class were sent to me because they had not passed the state reading test.

Establishing right relationship with students doesn't always come easy, especially with children who have had adults come in and out of their lives haphazardly. But developing a rapport and a right relationship with students can cut through many of the challenges they face. I wish I had been more thoughtful about this when I taught Xavier. Xavier was sent to me in seventh grade. I taught sixth, seventh, and eighth grade Title I Language Arts. All the students in my class were sent to me because they had not passed the state reading test.

I was unable to get Xavier to take anything seriously. He constantly acted up. It didn't matter if I tried to be nice, moved his seat, or fussed at him, I couldn't get him to take anything seriously. His presence in my class was a constant thorn in my side. I did not establish a proper relationship with him and he did not pass the state test.

The next year, I saw Xavier in the hallway in front of my classroom on the first day of school. I greeted him and we talked about what each of us did over the summer. I then noticed that the bell would be ringing shortly.

"Okay," I said, you better get to class. The bell's about to ring."

"I'm in your class!" he said with a smile.

"Ohhh, no you're not," I said, thinking he

was joking. "You've already had the Akua experience.

"Yes I am," he said holding up his class schedule with a priceless grin. "See, there's my name...and there's your name and room number!" he said quite pleased.

> What am I going to do with Xavier? I can't get him to take anything seriously?!

I was absolutely undone. "This cannot be," I thought to myself as he strolled nonchalantly into my classroom. During my planning time, I went to see the assistant principal who handled schedules.

"There's been a scheduling mistake," I told her. "Xavier is in my sixth period class."

"What's the mistake?" she asked.

"I had him last year in seventh grade."

"He didn't pass the state reading test, Mr. Akua. He must be in your class so that he can gain the skills to pass the test."

I politely and professionally agreed and excused myself from the office. I was upset.

"What am I going to do with Xavier?" I wondered. The problem was I really had never gotten to know him, until, of course, until November. In November, the school celebrated Red Ribbon Week which was supposed to be a time when students were taught about the perils of being involved with illegal drugs. I must admit that I hated Red Ribbon Week—it was because none of the lessons we were expected to teach on the subject were the least bit impactful.

"Just say no" was the witless mantra. No one questioned where the drugs came from or how they always ended up in the black community. No discussion of why black males who were caught with a small amount of crack cocaine received heavy prison sentences while white males who were caught with powdered cocaine often received parole and a slap on the wrist.

So I decided to use Red Ribbon Week as an opportunity to go deeper with my students and help them understand the system that caused and allowed drugs to fester in their community.

I showed my students an interview with "Freeway" Rick Ross, a black drug kingpin who franchised the drug trade in unprecedented fashion. Montel Williams interviewed him from a federal prison. I gave my students some questions to answer based on the interview.

Ross explained that he was first introduced to selling drugs by a teacher. He noted that he started making so much money, his finger tips were raw from counting. He began setting up crack houses around town, then went on the road to different cities setting up crack houses.

Ross further explained that he didn't realize the effect the drugs were having on the community until he noticed that his sister's kids were not properly dressed and had not been eating. They looked abandoned. He discovered that his own sister was strung out, but by then he was in too deep

Montel Williams asked Ross how he felt about all of the lives lost due to the drugs he sold. Ross confessed that he felt like the African chiefs who sold their own people into slavery.

I told the class we would discuss the interview tomorrow and to put their answers to the questions on the corner of my desk. We concluded class with our closing affirmation and the students filed out of class, except Xavier.

Xavier, eyes wide, deeply concerned, stood at my desk and looked like he had seen a ghost.

"Mr. Akua...that was deep," he said.

"What was deep?"

"The…the video..the interview," he said trying to explain.

"What was deep about it?" I asked.

"He said his own sister was strung out. He said he felt like an African chief who sold his own people into slavery," as if trying to teach me how important a proper understanding of the lesson was.

> "…my mother was strung out when she was pregnant with me," he said.

"We've talked about the perils of pushin' poison in our community. Why is it so deep to you now?"

Xavier's eyes dropped. Then he slowly looked back up at me.

"Because…my mother was strung out when she was pregnant with me."

"You know what that means don't you?" I asked.

"No…what?"

"You have to break the chains."

"What do you mean?" he asked.

"Are you still around drugs?"

"Yeah…everybody in my family is using. It's all around me."

"Do you want to be around it?"

"No!" he replied emphatically.

"Then you have to break the chains and not allow that into this generation. Remember, break the chains."

Those three words, "break the chains," became the new mantra between Xavier and me. When I saw him in the hall I would say, "break the chains." I would catch him at the door before class and whisper in his ear, "break the chains." Every paper I handed back to him had a number grade, a letter grade, and "break the chains."

From the day of that lesson, Xavier's behavior and performance changed dramatically. Prior to this, I had not developed a relationship with him. Tapping the affective domain in a relational manner allowed me to reach him. The rest of the year, he earned As and Bs, often asked to lead the Student Creed, and passed the sate reading test.

Questions for Thought, Reflection & Discussion

1. Discuss the Ten Nonverbal Questions Students Intuitively Ask Teachers.
2. Explain why everything hinges on relationship.
3. Examine and share your thoughts on the following statement: *"I have noticed that the one thing students want, but will never ask for is discipline."*

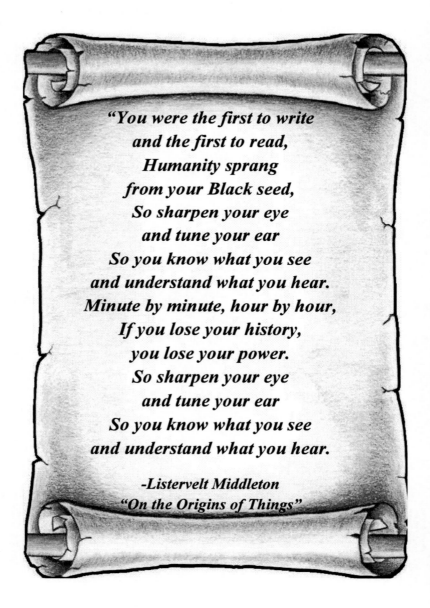

"You were the first to write
and the first to read,
Humanity sprang
from your Black seed,
So sharpen your eye
and tune your ear
So you know what you see
and understand what you hear.
Minute by minute, hour by hour,
If you lose your history,
you lose your power.
So sharpen your eye
and tune your ear
So you know what you see
and understand what you hear.

-Listervelt Middleton
"On the Origins of Things"

Chapter 9

Serving, Standing, and Shining as the Seba

The very construction of the word Seba, in its original form in the *medu netcher*, is very instructive about the duties and responsibilities of the Master Teacher. It should first be noted that the direct translation from *medu netcher* to English is spelled SBA. There is no "e," it is only added to facilitate ease of pronunciation.

The first glyph is a folded piece of cloth. It is the letter "s." The folded piece of cloth was often worm by women over the arm (Armah & Lam, 1997, p. 10). It was used for any number of activities including wiping or washing the mouth or nose of a child. This glyph represents *service*.

A Seba, a Master Teacher, is known for his/her service. (S)he is known to serve above and beyond the call of duty. (S)he is a nurturere of spirit and intellect. (S)he is known for coming in early and for staying late. (S)he claims all the children in his or her care. The Seba serves the children by looking beyond their faults and addressing their needs.

The second glyph in the construction of the word Seba is a leg "standing in a fixed position" (Armah & Lam, 1997, p. 22). It is the letter "b." This glyph represents the ability of the Seba to *stand*—to stand amidst the shifting sands of politics, policies, procedures, and paperwork. These can oftentimes be distractions to the essential work that must be done. Master Teachers are able to transcend politics, policies, procedures, and paperwork to truly meet the needs of the children.

The Seba is able to stand because (s)he does "not become weary in well-doing," (s)he is "steadfast, immovable, always abounding in the work" of transforming the lives of children.

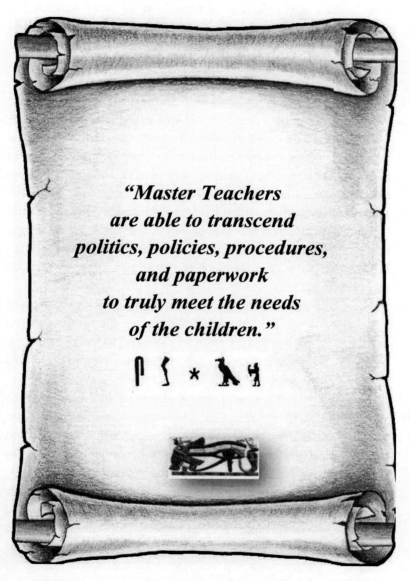

*"Master Teachers
are able to transcend
politics, policies, procedures,
and paperwork
to truly meet the needs
of the children."*

The third glyph in the word Seba is a star. It does not represent a letter. It is what is called a determinative. A determinative in *medu netcher* determines what the meaning of a word is beyond its phonetic construction. It puts the word in context. Remember, the Seba opens the door so the student may shine like a star.

First a Seba must *serve*. Second, a Seba must *stand*. Third, a Seba must *shine*. The power, spirit and energy that a Seba radiates is a compelling force. Seba are known to have a powerful presence that is filled with love, joy, peace, deep centeredness, reflection, wisdom, and insight. Just walking into a Seba's classroom causes a quickening of the spirit. The Seba shines and radiates transformative energy to all (s)he meets and knows. The children feel this energy. They long for it and are deeply attracted to it. They just want to be around the Seba. It is this energy that allows the Seba to "capture, inspire, and teach" them (Peters, 2008).

The fourth glyph in the word Seba is a vulture and it is the letter "a." The reason the vulture is used in the construction of the word Seba is because in ancient Kemet, the vulture was highly regarded because of its fierce protection of its young.

The Seba is a fierce protector of the young. The Seba provides a safe, secure, nurturing environment, whether in the classroom in the halls, in the cafeteria, on a field trip, etc. It doesn't matter where the students happen to be. In the presence of the Seba, there is safety, security and order.

The last glyph in the word Seba is another determinative. It is a scribe holding a palette and writing while standing. This represents *sharing* through active instruction. The Seba, because of his/her love for students, is willing to share of him/herself putting in extra hours of preparation, tutoring, mentoring, and teaching. The Seba is known to do whatever is necessary to meet the needs of the students.

In addition, the Seba is a master a active instruction. The energy they radiate compels children's attention and cooperation. But a Seba is skilled at differentiating instruction to match and meet students learning styles and intelligences. The glyph of the scribe writing also indicates perhaps that the Seba is very intentional about writing and documenting what works. This is something that Seba must do in order to advance the profession by people who get results rather than those who speculate, often with unproven policies and programs that do not serve the best interest of the children.

Another point worth mentioning is that the scribe is walking with the left foot forward. In Kemet (ancient Egypt) there are many statues of pharaohs with their left foot forward. This represents motion. Additionally, the movement of the left foot activates and stimulates the right brain which is deeply intuitive. Much of public school methods and information is left brain and analytical in nature. The Seba taps into the creative, spiritual, right brain in the midst of active instruction, thereby balancing it with left brain activities to promote and produce a well-developed and fully-functioning student.

While the construction of the word Seba (Master Teacher) is instructive, it is also important to note that the word for pupil or student was also *seba* and has a similar construction (Faulkner, 1962, p. 219). Notice that the word for student does not contain the determinatives.

What is a student in the ancient African conception? One who learns to *serve, stand,* and *shine.* The student seba learns to serve elders, family, community, and humanity. (S)he learns to stand on the morals, values, and principles that are in harmony with the best traditions of African people. The seba student learns to shine with the radiance of ancestral wisdom, strength, and self-determination. The student, seba, learns to serve, stand, and shine from the example of the Seba (Master Teacher).

Today, many students are unaware of their responsibility to serve, stand, and shine. Similarly, many teachers are unaware of their intrinsic duty to provide an example of the same. As teachers of African American students, we must center ourselves for the work ahead. We must walk with *Imani*, faith. Imani is the seventh principle of Kwanzaa and instructs us "to believe with all our hearts in our parents, teachers, leaders, and children, and in the righteousness and victory of our struggle" (Karenga, 1998). There must be a conscious and consistent determination among teachers to do *sankofa*, to return and retrieve *the best* of the culture. Recapture and rescue it from the hands of obscurity and hegemony, bring it to the children, and use it to uplift humanity.

SEBA

SERVE   SHARE
STAND   SECURE
SHINE

Armah, A. & Lam, A. M. (1997). *Hieroglyphics for babies.* Per Ankh: Senegal

Questions for Thought, Reflection & Discussion

1. Explain what the first character in the word Seba means.
2. Explain what the second character in the word Seba means.
3. Explain what the third character in the word Seba means.
4. How can the deeper meaning of the word Seba guide our role as educators? Explain.

Epilogue

James Baldwin's 1961 nonfictional essay, *A Talk to Teachers* begins:

> "…we are living through a very dangerous time…We are in a revolutionary situation, no matter how unpopular that word has become in this country. The society in which we live is desperately menaced, not [from without] but from within. So any citizen of this country who figures himself as responsible—and particularly those of you who deal with the minds and hearts of young people—must be prepared to 'go for broke'."

And in my study of Seba, Master Teachers around the country, "go for broke" is exactly what they do. Likewise, Dr. Carlos Azcoitia has observed, "You cannot be cautious and extraordinary at the same time."

The times we are living in require a consciousness, character, and commitment that goes far beyond what most schools and school systems require. To fully grasp what is necessary for those who teach to tap the spirit, touch the soul and transform lives forever, we must return to the source. For those who wish to take on the sage wisdom of Ptahhotep who observed that the Seba "feeds the soul with what endures," there must then be a deeper and higher understanding of what is expected.

This level of expectation has been culled and codified from the people of Kush (Ethiopia) and is embodied in the term *Jegna*. Jegna is an Ethiopian Amharic term for "the master teacher."

I was first introduced to Dr. Asa Hilliard's work by Dr. Leslie Fenwick, Dr. James C. Young, and Dr. Itihari Toure as I pursued graduate studies in education at Clark Atlanta

University. They insisted I review his work because they felt I was producing and demonstrating the very things he had been writing, researching, teaching, and demonstrating for decades. They also viewed his scholarly work as critical to my development as an educator. I would have lengthy conversations with each of them about Dr. Hilliard's work before I had the chance to meet him personally.

In 2003, I was initiated into The Jegna Collective, convened by Dr. Hilliard and a number of African-centered scholars and practitioners who have been deeply involved in the work of transforming children, parents, and communities for decades. Along with a number of other initiates, we were immersed in the best of the African tradition of education and transformation. We were blessed to spend hours in communication with profound scholars and healers who had a track record of excellence.

In 2005, Dr. Hilliard invited me to speak on the same platform with him at the National Alliance of Black School Educators (NABSE) Conference in Detroit. As he introduced me and welcomed me to the stage in front of the hundreds of educators present in his session, I asked him to remain on stage with me for a moment. I then made him a promise and asked the audience to repeat the promise with me to him. The promise was simply this: "We will continue what you have begun."

To continue the work of educational excellence and services to youth and communities, which was actually begun thousands of years ago in Africa, we must look at the qualities of the Jegna, which go hand in hand with that of the Seba.

1. They have been tested in struggle and battle.
2. They show extraordinary and unusual fearlessness.
3. They produce exceptionally high quality work.

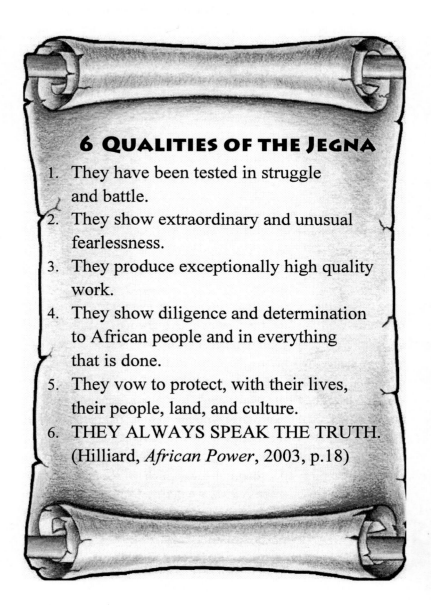

6 QUALITIES OF THE JEGNA

1. They have been tested in struggle and battle.
2. They show extraordinary and unusual fearlessness.
3. They produce exceptionally high quality work.
4. They show diligence and determination to African people and in everything that is done.
5. They vow to protect, with their lives, their people, land, and culture.
6. THEY ALWAYS SPEAK THE TRUTH. (Hilliard, *African Power*, 2003, p.18)

4. They show diligence and determination to African people and in everything that is done.
5. They vow to protect, with their lives, their people, land, and culture.
6. THEY ALWAYS SPEAK THE TRUTH. (Hilliard, *African Power*, 2003, p.18)

Further, Hilliard observes that "over and beyond technical excellence, they [Jegna] are deeply spiritual people....one informant from Ethiopia told me recently that he recalled that the Jegna was a person of the highest moral character and wisdom. He said that the Jegna, to them is a person who is as close as one can get to being like God" (Hilliard, *African Power*, 2003, p.19).

Understanding and demonstrating the qualities of the Jegna could be a class and separate book in and of themselves. Each of the six characteristics indicate a level of self-determination, resilience, and resolve that we must recapture if we are to reach and teach Black children, and indeed, all children. It's not optional, it's *essential*.

It is clear that teaching is more than just a job. It's even more than a career. It is a *calling*—a critical calling which compels one ot accept a mighty mission with a powerful purpose. Few teachers have had the opportunity to be under the tutelage of a Master Teacher or to carefully observe a Master Teacher at work for an impactful period of time. As a result, many educators have been lulled to sleep, complacently accepting the notion that underachievement for Black children is normal, understandable and acceptable.

I took my promise to Baba Asa very seriously that cold winter day in Detroit at NABSE, though I had no idea the breadth and depth of his contributions as an educator, psychologist, former superintendent, forensic examiner, historian, husband, and father, to name a few.

I have traveled the country speaking in 35+ cities, doing 80+ presentations for the past six years to students, parents and teachers. It is exhausting, but exhilarating work—a true labor of love. It has been quite an experience getting a panoramic view of American education, then seeing how African American educators, parents, and students navigate through this labyrinth. I am now more ready to than ever to continue to assist in taking education to the level that we know is possible. Please join me on the journey.

References

Akbar, Na'im (1998). *Know thyself.* Mind Productions & Associates, Tallahassee, Florida.

Armah, A. & Lam, A.M. (1997). *Hieroglyphics for babies: A drawing and writing manual for preschoolers, parents, and teachers.* Per Ankh: Senegal.

Browder, Anthony (1992). *Nile valley contributions to civilization.* Institute of Karmic Guidance: Washington, D.C.

Akua, Chike (2001). *A treasure within: Stories of remembrance & Rediscovery,* Imani Enterprises: Conyers, GA.

Akua, Chike (2001). *A treasure within: Parent/teacher resource guide,* Imani Enterprises, Conyers, GA.

Akua, Chike and Stephens, Tavares (2006). *Reading revolution: Reconnecting the Roots,* Imani Enterprises, Conyers, GA.

Akua, Chike (2004). *A Kwanzaa awakening: Lessons for the Community* (4th Edition), Imani Enterprises, Conyers, GA.

Akua, Chike (2005). *Words of power: Ancient insights & modern messages for parents, teachers, and students,* Imani Enterprises, Conyers, GA.

Ani, Marimba (1980). *Let the circle be unbroken: Implications for African spirituality in the Diaspora.* NY: Nkonimfo Publications.

Clarke, John H. (1991). Notes for an African world revolution: Africans at the crossroads. Trenton, NJ: Africa World Press.

Delpit, Lisa (1995). *Other people's children: cultural conflict in the classroom.* NY: The New Press.

Faulkner, Raymond (1962). *A concise dictionary of middle Egyptian.* Oxford: Griffith Insitutte.

Fenwick, Leslie (2001). *Patterns of excellence: policy perspectives on diversifying teaching and school leadership.* Atlanta, GA: Southern Education Foundation.

Finch, Charles (1998). *The star of deep beginnings: The African genesis of science and technology.* Atlanta, GA: Khenti Press.

Fu-Kiau, Kimbwadende Kia Bunseki (1991). *Self-healing power and therapy.* NY: Vantage Press.

Fultz, Michael (2004). The displacement of Black educators post-Brown: An overview and analysis," *History of Education Quarterly* 44 (Spring 2004): 11-45.

Gallman, B. Ani, M., Williams, O. (2004). *To be African: Essays by Africans in the process of sankofa: returning to our source of power.* Atlanta, GA: M.A.A.T., Inc.

Hale, Janice (1982). *Black children:Their roots, culture, and learning styles.* Baltimore: Johns Hopkins University Press.

Hilliard, A., Williams, L. & Damali, N. (1987). The teachings of Ptahhotep: The oldest book in the world. Atlanta, GA: Blackwood Press.

Hilliard, Asa (1997). *SBA: The reawakening of the African mind.* Tallahassee, Florida: Makare Publishing.

Hilliard, Asa (2003). *African power: Affirming African indigenous socialization in the face of culture wars.* Tallahassee, FL: Makare Publishing.

Karenga, Maulana (1998): *Kwanzaa: A celebration of family, community, and culture.* Los Angeles, CA: University of Sankore Press.

King, Joyce E. (1991). Dysconscious racism: Ideology, Identity, and the Miseducation of Teachers. *Journal of Negro Education, 60,* 133.

King, Joyce E. (1992). Diaspora literacy and consciousness in the struggle against miseducation in the Black community. *Journal of Negro Education, 61,* 317-340.

King, Joyce E. (2005). *Black education: A transformative research and action agenda for the new century.* Mahwah, NJ: Lawrence Erlbaum Associates.

Ladson-Billings, Gloria (1994). *Dreamkeepers: Successful teachers of African American students.* San Francisco, CA: Jossey-Bass Publishers.

Ladson-Billings, Gloria (1995). Toward a theory of culturally relevant pedagogy. *American Educational Research Journal, 32,* 465-491.

Middleton, Listervelt (2003). *True of voice: The poetry of Listervelt Middleton,* Gainesville, FL: Makare Publishing.

Murrell, Peter (2009). Identity, agency, and culture: Black achievement and educational attainment. In *The Sage Handbook of African American Education,* pp 89-105, Ed. By Linda Tillman.

ᴨ ∫ ⋆ 𝄡

Obenga, Theophile (2002). *Imhotep Magazine*. San Francisco, CA: San Francisco State University Press.

Perry, T., Steele, C., Hilliard, A. (2003). *Young, gifted, and Black: Promoting high achievement among African American students*. Boston: Beacon Press.

Peters, Stephen (2008). *Teaching to capture and inspire all learners*. Thousand Oaks, CA: Corwin Press.

Shockley, Kmt (2008). *The miseducation of Black children*. Chicago: African American Images.

Shujaa, Mwalimu (1994). Too much schooling, too little education: a paradox of Black life in White societies. Trenton, NJ: Africa World Press.

Siddle-Walker, Vanessa (2000). Valued segregated schools for African American children in the South, 1935-1969: A Review of Common Themes and Characteristics," *Review of Educational Research 70*, 253-285.

Some, Sobonfu (1997). *The spirit of intimacy: Ancient teachings in the ways of relationships*. Berkeley, CA: Berkeley Hill Books

Swanson, Anna (2003). *Dr. John Henrik Clarke: his life, his words, his works*. Atlanta, GA: I AM Unlimited Publishing.

Wilkerson, Kobie (2008). *Fred and Mary*. Love II Learn Books.

Wilson, Amos (1991). *Awakening the genius in Black children*. NY: Afrikan World Infosystems.

Woodson, Carter G. (1933). *The mis-education of the Negro.* Washington, D.C.: Associated Publishers.

About Chike Akua

Mr. Chike Akua has been called "an educational revolutionary." He is the founding organizer and executive director of the Teacher Transformation Institute, a standards-based, research-driven, best practices training conference for teachers. Mr. Akua is a leading authority on increasing the achievement of today's students, especially those that many teachers find most challenging. As recognized master teacher, Mr. Akua has been an invited keynote presenter at regional and national conferences, school systems, colleges and universities. With a culturally relevant approach toward closing the achievement gap, he is known for his dynamic, interactive presentations to teachers, parents, and students.

Mr. Akua has 14 years of teaching experience in Virginia and Georgia public school systems. In 1995, he was selected **Teacher of the Year** for Newport News Public Schools (VA) and was also selected as one of *Ebony* magazine's **"50 Leaders of Tomorrow."** A year later, in 1996, the Dekalb County Board of Education (Atlanta, Georgia) recognized him with the Excellence in Education Award for Service to Youth. Additionally, he has been an invited lecturer for undergraduate and graduate courses in teacher education at Georgia State University and Clark Atlanta University.

Deeply committed to culturally relevant pedagogy and the development of culturally relevant instructional materials, Mr. Akua has written and published several books and parent/teacher guides designed for today's students. His book, *A Treasure Within: Stories of Remembrance and Rediscovery* was nominated for the **NAACP Image Award**. *Reading Revolution* is his most recent publication (co-authored with Tavares Stephens). The books have been adopted by the Georgia Department of Juvenile Justice Regional Youth Detention Center and public schools around the country.

Mr. Akua earned the Master of Arts degree in education with a concentration in school counseling from **Clark Atlanta University** and is a *cum laude* graduate of **Hampton University** where he earned the bachelor of arts degree in education (concentration in English Education).

Mr. Akua is a committed volunteer with several youth mentoring and leadership academies and college preparatory camps for middle school and high school students. He has helped lead over 1000 students and parents on trips throughout Egypt and Ghana through the **D'Zert Club's Teen Summit 1000** program. Mr. Akua is frequently called upon by education, civic, and social organizations to speak about educational excellence and cultural knowledge.

To book Chike Akua for a conference keynote speech, *Teacher Transformation!* workshop, *ParentPower!* presentation, *African Origins!* or *SexceptionalAbstinence!* or *SuccessQuest!* presentation for students, email akua@bellsouth.net or call 770-309-6664.

Books, DVDs, and Posters
by Chike Akua

> **Order books, posters, and DVDs at**
> **www.MyTeacherTransformation.com**

Education for Transformation: The Keys to Releasing the Genius of African American Students
By Chike Akua

This book details African-centered and culturally relevant instructional strategies used with some of the most challenging students during Mr. Akua's fourteen years as a public school teacher.

It also documents the most promising practices of Master Teachers he has observed around the country.

Praise for *Education for Transformation:*

"*Chike Akua has done a masterful job in his latest book,* Education for Transformation. *As one of his student's wrote, 'most teachers teach from the book, but you teach from the heart.'*"
-Dr. Jawanza Kunjufu, Author
There's Nothing Wrong With Black Students

"*This book is a must-read for all serious educators who want to get results and understand the connection between culture and achievement.*"
Dr. Joyce E. King, Benjamin E. Mays Chair
Georgia State University

Black History Power Pak!
By Chike Akua

The Black History Power Pak is a collection of 6 books by Chike Akua, 2 African Origins DVDs and a bonus DVD about how you can earn a FREE trip to Egypt.

The Black History Power Pak is a wonderful way to supplement your current lessons because it is a curriculum of correction and inclusion. Use to it show your students the beauty of African and African American culture and contributions. Increase and improve reading comprehension, cultural awareness, and character development.

For a description of each of the books and DVDs included, see the following pages.

Reading Revolution: Reconnecting the Roots

By Chike Akua & Tavares Stephens

A collection of 90 reading selections about African and African American people of extraordinary accomplishment. Use *Reading Revolution* to improve reading comprehension and cultural consciousness at the same time:

- Standardized test format with multiple choice questions
- Topic, main idea, supporting details and sequencing
- Vocabulary development and context clues
- Making inferences and drawing conclusions

"Chike Akua and Tavares Stephens combine excellent teaching skills, deep knowledge of African history and culture, and, as master teachers, a real grasp of students' interests and thinking. Reading Revolution *is an outstanding product of this mixture, and hence a rare value for schools."*

Asa G. Hilliard III-Nana Baffour Amankwatia II, Ed.D.
Fuller E. Calloway Professor of Urban Education
Georgia State University

"At a time when teachers across the nation are struggling to find the delicate balance between curricular standards and meaningful content that students will readily identify with, Mr. Akua and Mr. Stephens have definitely hit the mark with Reading Revoltion."

Vonzia Phillips, Ph.D., Director of Premiere Middle Schools
Dekalb County Schools
Atlanta, GA

Chike Akua and Tavares Stephens have crafted a masterful publication which makes reading, vocabulary building and comprehension memorable learning experiences."

Anthony T. Browder, Author
Nile Valley Contributions to Civilization

A Treasure Within: Stories of Remembrance & Rediscovery

"What would it be like to meet an ancient African Ancestor? Marcus, Imani, and Daniel are about to find out! A treasure Within is a book of three short stories in which young people have encounters with ancient African ancestors to learn about traditional African morals, values, history, and culture.

"A Treasure Within *is the book that many of us have been waiting for. The deep thinking of Ancient African is grasped and communicated clearly through these three powerful stories. Families, counselors, teachers,, students, and the community, in general, can relate directly to these stories...I am thankful for this outstanding contribution to our mental and spiritual liberation. Our Ancestors are pleased. Amun is satisfied."*

Asa G. Hilliard III – Nana Baffour Amankwatia II, Ed.D.

Fuller E. Calloway Professor of Urban Education
Georgia State University

"Chike Akua, a master teacher, engages the reader with three compelling stories. His mastery of the written word intertwined with historical facts and cultural revelations invites the reader to be totally immersed. Readers of all ages will enjoy this literary rites of passage."

Phyllis Daniel
Middle School Principal

A   Treasure   Within: Parent/Teacher Resource Guide

This book is a complete companion curriculum to *A Treasure Within: Stories of Remembrance & Rediscovery*. It includes a wide range of activities to reinforce content objectives and develop character, cultural awareness, and commitment.

"...for teachers and parents who believe that classrooms and homes are places where the child's spirit is cultivated and soars, A Treasure Within: Stories of Remembrance & Rediscovery *and the accompanying* Parent/Teacher Resource Guide *provides a path – a path to knowledge and understanding."*

> Leslie T. Fenwick, Ph.D.
> Professor Of Educational Policy, Clark Atlanta University
> Visiting Scholar, Harvard School of Education

"A Treasure Within is a remarkable collection of stories with a broad appeal to all youth. The stories instruct, develop moral character, and entertain at the same time. The accompanying Parent/Teacher Resource Guide *is a great and useful addition to this wonderful collection."*

> Dr. William Hammond, Reading Instruction Coordinator
> Dekalb County School,
> Atlanta, Georgia

A Kwanzaa Awakening: Lessons for the Community

A Kwanzaa Awakening is a resource with activities for everyone. Parents, educators, and clergy will find activities for children K-12 and beyond. It includes:
- A Brief History of Kwanzaa
- Kwanzaa Classroom Activities (grades 6-12)
- Lessons for the Little Ones (K-5)
- A 3-act Play
- Worksheets and Puzzles
- Quiz and Test
- Coloring Activities
- Writing Activities
- Poetry
- Reading Comprehension Selections
- Kwanzaa in Christ: How to Celebrate Kwanzaa in the Church
- Kwanzaa and the Qu'ran: Islamic Expressions of the Seven Principles
- Glossary

"Through this book, Akua provides ways for us to value the lives of our children and ways to teach them who they are as children with a rich African heritage. This book...challenges us to train our children in ways that will affirm our past and secure our future."
James C. Anyike, M.Div.
Author, *African American Holidays*

Words of Power: Ancient Insights and Modern Messages for Parents, Teachers & Students **By Chike Akua**

This book contains almost two hundreds quotes and proverbs from African people and powerful people all over the world. Additionally it contains fill-in worksheets so that students can engage in a words of wisdom scavenger hunt.

Share the mother wit and wisdom that many of our children today are missing as you examine and interpret firurative language, simile and metaphor.

Sexceptional: The Ultimate and Essentail Teen Guide to Abstinence

By Chike Akua

Sexceptional is an adjective that describes "one who is willing to undertake the discipline, devotion, and determination to abstain from sexual activity until marriage." It takes an exceptional person because there are many weapons of mass distraction and weapons of mass deception. We hear a lot about safe sex, but abstinence is, hands down, the safest alternative. But when abstinence is mentioned, oftentimes young people are not given the tools to make abstinence work. This book is a tool box of insights and strategies.

The African Origins of Writing & Mathematics DVD
African Sacred Science DVD (Recorded LIVE!)

By Chike Akua

These dynamic and revealing DVDs give students an understanding of Africa's contributions to reading and writing, language and literature, science and technology, math and medicine, and so much more! A picture is worth a thousand words and these DVDs visually document African excellence, achievement, and ingenuity—ancient and modern.

The African Origins Empowerment Pak
By Chike Akua

The package includes five African Origins DVDs which visually document the history of Africans from ancient times to the present. It also includes a *BONUS* CD of Chike Akua's presentation at the Pan-African Student Leadership Conference and a copy of the book *The African Origins of Our Faith*.

Black History Poster Pak!
By Chike Akua
*Purchase the whole Pak for your school and get one <u>FREE</u>!

These beautiful, full-size, color posters on the following pages are both inspirational and instructional. They are a wonderful addition to any classroom, office or living room. Developed and designed by award-winning educator and author, Chike Akua, these posters are a rich resource for creating a culture of excellence and achievement in your classroom or school.

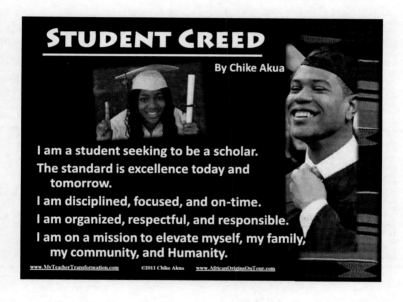

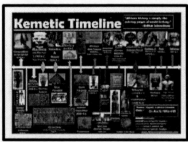

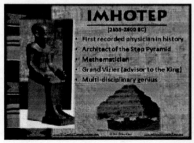

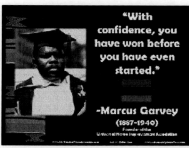

"Black people,... we are an *awesome* people. We have overcome every challenge that we have faced in history. Now, we must unite and spend our money with each other *consistently*, so that <u>WEALTH</u> will top the list of our triumphs."

-Delxino Wilson de Briano

www.BlackBusinessNetwork.com

"It's time that we, as Black people, take control of our future. By creating our own businesses and supporting them, we can do this!"

-Deborah Wilson de Briano
Vice President
TAG TEAM Marketing International, Inc.
& Co-Creator of
The Black Business Network
www.BlackBusinessNetwork.com

"There is a feminine as well as masculine side to truth (and) these are related not as inferior and superior, not as better or worse, not as weaker or stronger, but as complements— complements in one necessary and symmetric whole."

-Anna Julia Cooper
educator, author, activist, scholar
(1858-1964)

"Our crowns have been bought and paid for...All we have to do is put them on our heads."

-James Baldwin
Writer & Civil Rights Activist
(1924-1987)

"African history is simply the missing pages of *world* history."

-Arthur Schomburg
Historian & Archivist
(1874-1938)

AFRICAN PEOPLE MASTERED MATHEMATICS THOUSANDS OF YEARS AGO, AND TAUGHT THE WORLD!

MENTUHOTEP
CIRCA 2040 B.C.E.

Mentuhotep was a 12th Dynasty King of Kemet (Egypt) who ushered in the Literary Age, an age of productive and prolific writing which further documented the incredible accomplishments of the people of Kemet.

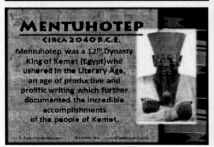

Order books, posters, and DVDs at
www.MyTeacherTransformation.com